NEW DIRECTIONS FOR YOUTH DEVELOPMENT

Theory
Practice
Research

summer | 2011

Recreation as a Developmental Experience

Lawrence R. Allen
Robert J. Barcelona

issue
editors

Gil G. Noam
Editor-in-Chief

JOSSEY-BASS™
An Imprint of

RECREATION AS A DEVELOPMENTAL EXPERIENCE
Lawrence R. Allen, Robert J. Barcelona (eds.)
New Directions for Youth Development, No. 130, Summer 2011
Gil G. Noam, Editor-in-Chief
This is a peer-reviewed journal.

Microfilm copies of issues and articles are available in 16mm and 35mm, as well as microfiche in 105mm, through University Microfilms Inc., 300 North Zeeb Road, Ann Arbor, MI 48106-1346.

New Directions for Youth Development is indexed in Academic Search (EBSCO), Academic Search Premier (EBSCO), Contents Pages in Education (T&F), Current Abstracts (EBSCO), Educational Research Abstracts Online (T&F), EMBASE/Excerpta Medica (Elsevier), ERIC Database (Education Resources Information Center), Index Medicus/MEDLINE/PubMed (NLM), MEDLINE/PubMed (NLM), SoclNDEX (EBSCO), Sociology of Education Abstracts (T&F), and Studies on Women & Gender Abstracts (T&F).

NEW DIRECTIONS FOR YOUTH DEVELOPMENT (ISSN 1533-8916, electronic ISSN 1537-5781) is part of the Jossey-Bass Psychology Series and is published quarterly by Wiley Subscription Services, Inc., A Wiley Company, at Jossey-Bass, 989 Market Street, San Francisco, CA 94103-1741. POSTMASTER: Send address changes to New Directions for Youth Development, Jossey-Bass, 989 Market Street, San Francisco, CA 94103-1741.

SUBSCRIPTIONS for individuals cost $89.00 for U.S./Canada/Mexico; $113.00 international. For institutions, agencies, and libraries, $265.00 U.S.; $305.00 Canada/Mexico; $339.00 international. Prices subject to change. Refer to the order form that appears at the back of most volumes of this journal.

EDITORIAL CORRESPONDENCE should be sent to the Editor-in-Chief, Dr. Gil G. Noam, McLean Hospital, Harvard Medical School, 115 Mill Street, Belmont, MA 02478.

Cover photograph by Blend_Images/iStockphoto

www.josseybass.com

Contents

Issue Editors' Notes

RECENT ATTENTION IN both the popular press and the research literature has highlighted many of the consequences of a lack of active, meaningful leisure participation in the lives of youth, particularly when school is not in session. For example, juvenile crime rates in the unsupervised hours immediately following school are higher than at other times of the day.[1] In addition, research indicates that youth spend an average of fifty-three hours each week using electronic media, yet participation in free-time outdoor activities is on the decline.[2] While this decline in participation may be indicative of a lack of opportunity for some youth, particularly those from low-income families,[3] many young people are no longer choosing to participate in engaging, healthy, and physically active leisure opportunities.[4] It is perhaps not surprising, then, that youth physical activity levels are alarmingly low and obesity rates among children and adolescents are on the rise.[5]

The recreation field has a rich history in providing programs, services, and activities for youth. For recreation professionals working on the ground with youth, there remains little doubt that their programs contribute to their participants' well-being. However, one of the challenges that the field has faced is the general perception that recreation experiences are discretionary, frivolous, or nonessential, and thus they are vulnerable from the perspective of public and other forms of community funding. To counter this perception, research efforts in the 1990s focused on the role of recreation programs and services in building resiliency and protective factors for primarily at-risk youth populations.[6] However, the growing emphasis in the past decade on positive youth development has helped to reshape the research direction to one focused

NEW DIRECTIONS FOR YOUTH DEVELOPMENT, NO. 130, SUMMER 2011 © WILEY PERIODICALS, INC.
Published online in Wiley Online Library (wileyonlinelibrary.com) • DOI: 10.1002/yd.392

on recreation from both a primary prevention and a strengths-based approach.[7]

While the broader public may still view recreation programs as "fun and games," a growing body of research suggests that recreation activities can be powerful developmental contexts when they are properly framed and intentionally designed. This volume highlights much of that research, and the articles that follow provide ample evidence that well-framed recreation activities and contexts can provide a range of positive developmental outcomes, including autonomous action, freedom of expression, intrinsic reward, initiative, creativity, prolonged engagement, identity formation, development of competence, enhanced physical and emotional health, and a sense of belongingness.

Youth development continues to be a priority for both practitioners and researchers in the recreation field. The National Recreation and Park Association continues to keep youth development as a major strategic initiative, and it recently commissioned a white paper by Peter Witt and Linda Caldwell (two of the authors in this special issue): *The Rationale for Recreation Services for Youth: An Evidence Based Approach.*[8] Similarly, the American Camp Association's ongoing efforts to document the outcomes of organized camp experiences have led to the creation of new and robust youth development measurement tools.[9] In addition, special issues devoted to youth development have been featured numerous times in the *Journal of Park and Recreation Administration* and the *Therapeutic Recreation Journal.*[10] Recreation as a potential lever for development is also getting attention from major funders, such as the Robert Wood Johnson Foundation's Active Living Research program.

This issue of *New Directions for Youth Development* builds on this foundation by exploring the importance of meaningful recreation and leisure experiences in the lives of youth and the value of recreation from a developmental perspective. It focuses on the developmental potential of specific recreation contexts and settings and provides research and evidence-based strategies outlining the activities that best promote positive youth development. Finally, it demonstrates how recreation is being used to strengthen individual and community assets and its role as a contributor in addressing pressing social issues. The first article provides the platform for examining how and under what conditions play, recreation, and leisure contribute to adolescent development. The second through seventh articles highlight various leisure and recreation contexts: the family, schools, the community, nature, camp, and adventure programs. The eighth article focuses on the competencies and professional development of recreation and youth development staff. The final article examines the intersection of recreation and public policy and provides an exhortation for the field to more effectively reframe and reposition itself to gain traction with key funders and policymakers.

We thank all of the issue contributors for their hard work and dedication to research and professional practice in recreation: Linda L. Caldwell, Peter A. Witt, Peter J. Ward, Ramon B. Zabriskie, David S. Fleming, Corliss Outley, Jason N. Bocarro, Chris T. Boleman, Barry A. Garst, Laurie P. Browne, M. Deborah Bialeschki, Fran P. Mainella, Joel R. Agate, Brianna S. Clark, Jim Sibthorp, Cass Morgan, Amy R. Hurd, Jennifer A. Bruggeman, and Phillip Lovell. We also thank Erin Cooney and Gil Noam for their support and assistance in preparing this issue and the anonymous peer reviewers who provided invaluable and useful feedback on the initial drafts. A growing body of evidence links recreation and youth development. This issue of *New Directions for Youth Development* brings some of it under one cover.

Lawrence R. Allen
Robert J. Barcelona
Editors

Notes

1. Snyder, H., & Sickmund, M. (2006). *Juvenile offenders and victims: 2006 National Report*. Washington, DC: Office of Juvenile Justice and Delinquency Prevention.

2. Rideout, V., Foehr, U., & Roberts, D. (2010). *Generation M: Media in the lives of 8 to 18 year olds*. Menlo Park, CA: Kaiser Family Foundation; Louv, R.

(2005). *Last child in the woods: Saving our children from nature-deficit disorder.* Chapel Hill, NC: Algonquin Books.

3. Quinn, J. (1999). Where need meets opportunity: Youth development programs for early teens. *Future of Children, 9*(2), 96–116.

4. Louv. (2005).

5. Centers for Disease Control and Prevention. (2009). Youth risk behavior surveillance–United States, 2009. *Morbidity and Mortality Weekly Report, 59*(SS-5), 1–142; Ogden, C. L., Carroll, M. D., & Flegal, K. M. (2008). High body mass index for age among US children and adolescents, 2003–2006. *Journal of the American Medical Association, 299*(20), 2401–2405.

6. Allen, L. A., Stevens, B., & Harwell, R. (1996). Benefits-based management activity planning model for youth in at-risk environments. *Journal of Park and Recreation Administration, 14*(3), 10–19; Witt, P. A., & Crompton, J. L. (1996). The at-risk youth recreation project. *Journal of Park and Recreation Administration, 14*(3), 1–9.

7. Caldwell, L. L. (2000). Beyond fun and games? Challenges to adopting a prevention and youth development approach to youth recreation. *Journal of Park and Recreation Administration, 18*(3), 1–18.

8. Witt, P. A., & Caldwell, L. (2010). *The rationale for recreation services for youth: An evidenced based approach.* Reston, VA: National Recreation and Park Association.

9. Ellis, G., & Sibthorp, J. (2006). *Development and validation of a battery of age-appropriate measures for camper outcomes.* Martinsville, IN: American Camp Association.

10. Bocarro, J. N., Greenwood, P. B., & Henderson, K. A. (2008). An integrative review of youth development research in selected United States recreation journals. *Journal of Park and Recreation Administration, 26*(2), 4–27.

LAWRENCE R. ALLEN *is the dean of the College of Health, Education, and Human Development at Clemson University.*

ROBERT J. BARCELONA *is an assistant professor of youth development leadership and Department of Parks, Recreation and Tourism Management at Clemson University.*

Executive Summary

Chapter One: Leisure, recreation, and play from a developmental context

Linda L. Caldwell, Peter A. Witt

Participation in activities and experiences defined as play, recreation, and leisure has important developmental implications for youth. Elements and characteristics of leisure experiences contribute directly to the development of identity, autonomy, competence, initiative, civic duty, and social connections. Whether in informal or formal, appropriately structured and organized programs, leisure experiences can help facilitate adolescent development in these areas. For example, one of the defining elements of leisure is that it is characterized by free choice and self-determination. Programs that promote leadership, choice, autonomy, and initiative can help adolescents deal with developmental challenges associated with this age group. Leisure experiences can also promote civic engagement and provide important peer-to-peer, peer-to-adult, and peer-to-community connections. The social context of leisure is important to adolescent development in that it provides opportunities to learn empathy, loyalty, and intimacy in their group activities, as well as to negotiate with peers, resolve conflict, and work together for communal goals. In addition, adolescents often report positive emotional experiences in leisure, which can serve as a relief from the stress they feel in other areas of their lives and contribute to positive psychological adjustment and well-being. A case study is used to show how planned, purposive

NEW DIRECTIONS FOR YOUTH DEVELOPMENT, NO. 130, SUMMER 2011 © WILEY PERIODICALS, INC.
Published online in Wiley Online Library (wileyonlinelibrary.com) • DOI: 10.1002/yd.393

programs can be used as critical components of efforts to contribute to adolescent development.

Chapter Two: Positive youth development within a family leisure context: Youth perspectives of family outcomes

Peter J. Ward, Ramon B. Zabriskie

Although a variety of recreation programs provide valuable settings for youth development and should continue, the home should be considered the first and perhaps the most essential context for positive youth development. Family leisure experiences are purposively or intentionally planned by invested adults (parents) to create and maintain meaningful relationships and provide supportive opportunities for their children to learn skills and develop behaviors that will not only strengthen current family life but ultimately contribute to their overall positive development. The article presents family leisure research from a youth perspective and sets out the implications of the role of home-based core types of leisure that families engage in.

Chapter Three: Back to the future: The potential relationship between leisure and education

David S. Fleming, Lawrence R. Allen, Robert J. Barcelona

There is a long, documented history of the relationships among leisure, recreation, and education dating back to Greek philosophy. Originally there was little differentiation among the terms as they were presented as a unified process for youth and human development. Over time, each of these fields has developed, and their definitions have been shaped and reshaped. Using some of the original conceptions from Aristotle and Plato, coupled with foundational premises suggested by Dewey, this article frames current youth development efforts in a historical context. The authors suggest that perhaps what the separate professions might define as high-quality leisure, recreation, and educational experiences still maintain links among each. They further suggest that planned experiences with increasing levels of coordination can strengthen these links and develop an "education-for-leisure" perspective among participating youth and the choices they make. Self-determination theory (SDT) refers to the autonomy in choosing a particular behavior or action. Youth development opportunities that make connections between the content of a regular school day and choice of activity during out-of-school time can inculcate self-determined leisure choices that are productive. Planned and intentional educational experiences expand the possibilities for productive recreational choices. This article therefore proposes a framework for increasing levels of coordination among educational and recreational entities so that participating youth can develop and adopt an education-for-leisure disposition.

Chapter Four: Recreation as a component of the community youth development system

Corliss Outley, Jason N. Bocarro, Chris T. Boleman

In an era of fragmented school systems and budget cuts, many educators and youth leaders seeking to solve the problems that youth face are turning to out-of-school-time programs. In many communities, these programs are seen as essential in the development of youth into fully functioning adults. One such area of the out-of-school-time sector is the provision of recreation services. Recreational services have a vital role in connecting youth to their communities, as well as enabling youth and adult allies to improve challenging conditions. This chapter outlines the historical role that recreation has played in community youth development programs and shows how community youth development has evolved. It then looks at how organizations in three communities—

NEW DIRECTIONS FOR YOUTH DEVELOPMENT • DOI: 10.1002/yd

the Youthline Outreach Mentorship program in Minneapolis, a 4-H initiative in Parker City, Texas, and the Hockey Is for Everyone program—have successfully applied the theoretical knowledge. Best practices from these programs illustrate that the role of recreation in community youth development is changing. No longer are recreation programs about providing just "fun and games." Recreation organizations are now placing more value on the development of the community as a whole, in addition to the individual well-being of young people.

Chapter Five: Youth development and the camp experience

Barry A. Garst, Laurie P. Browne, M. Deborah Bialeschki

The organized camp experience has been an important part of the lives of children, youth, and adults for over 150 years. The camp experience is a way for young people to explore and search for an authenticity often missing in other parts of their lives that contributes to their healthy transition into adulthood. Over the past decade, tremendous growth in the volume and rigor of camp-related research has occurred, facilitated by a targeted research agenda conducted by the American Camp Association. This agenda was founded on three national research projects conducted between 2003 and 2007: a study to identify the developmental outcomes of the camp experience, a benchmarking study of the youth development supports and opportunities provided through camp experiences, and a program improvement project directed toward enhancing supports and opportunities provided by camps. The findings from these research projects suggest that camp experiences promote developmental outcomes in both campers and staff and that camps provide the supports and opportunities needed for positive youth development. This article explores the developmental outcomes of the camp experience and

NEW DIRECTIONS FOR YOUTH DEVELOPMENT • DOI: 10.1002/yd

the characteristics of the supports and opportunities afforded by camp experiences, including settings, structures, and programs and activities, as a way to provide a clearer understanding of camp as a positive youth development setting. Innovations and opportunities in research related to the provision of quality camp experiences are also considered.

Chapter Six: Outdoor-based play and reconnection to nature: A neglected pathway to positive youth development

Fran P. Mainella, Joel R. Agate, Brianna S. Clark

Throughout history, outdoor-based play and the connection to nature have been recognized as important contributors to a happy life and healthy development. At times, however, play and nature have been neglected and viewed as frivolous and wasteful. In the early twentieth century, the first play movement took place to get children out of the factories and back outdoors to play. Now, a century later, factors including twenty-four-hour media, stranger danger, and overscheduling of children's time have resulted in a level of play deprivation that is contributing to a host of social, emotional, and physical problems. This article draws on recent research that shows that as many as 40 percent of America's schools have eliminated or significantly reduced recess. Also, children and adolescents are spending an average of fifty-three hours each week in front of screen media, and only 31 percent of mothers report that their children play outside as frequently as they did as children. The deficits in outdoor-based play that arise from these lifestyles have resulted in significant increases in emotional and psychological disorders, decreased capacity to deal with stressors, and decreased physical fitness. This article describes specific organizations and programs that address the problem of play deprivation and reconnection to the outdoors.

NEW DIRECTIONS FOR YOUTH DEVELOPMENT • DOI: 10.1002/yd

Chapter Seven: Adventure-based programming: Exemplary youth development practice

Jim Sibthorp, Cass Morgan

Despite functioning on the periphery of academic scholarship, theory development, and rigorous science, the better adventure-based programs are functioning at the forefront of professional youth practices. This article links the core elements and processes of adventure programs to the literature on positive youth development and quality youth programming. Contemporary work on developmental systems theory, developmental cascades, and initiative are well aligned with the historical, philosophical, and programmatic roots of adventure education. In addition, adventure programs afford some powerful experiences by way of distinct features such as isolation, dosage, different physical environments, holistic approaches, social experiences, and program novelty. This combination of features often provides a microcosm for youth to live, learn, experiment, and grow. Despite the strengths in prototypical adventure programs, they remain less accessible and are not easily delivered to many youth. Although there are clearly differences in adventure program and other youth activities, many of the qualities of adventure programs can be included in a broader and more accessible spectrum of youth opportunities. This article thus explains the congruency between the literature on positive youth development and adventure programs and generalizes current tenets of adventure programs to the broader context of youth practice. It is time to recognize the important role that adventure programs play for many youth and fully embrace what these diverse and successful programs can teach the general field of positive youth development.

NEW DIRECTIONS FOR YOUTH DEVELOPMENT • DOI: 10.1002/yd

Chapter Eight: *A competency-based approach to preparing staff as recreation and youth development leaders*

Robert J. Barcelona, Amy R. Hurd, Jennifer A. Bruggeman

Youth development professionals and parks and recreation professionals often are charged with providing services to youth. However, the approach of each can be quite different as recreation is a primary focus for recreation professionals and part of many services offered by youth development specialists. Despite the differences, these two groups of professionals can learn a great deal from each other. This article examines youth development and staff training with examples from the field and suggests how youth development professionals can learn from recreation professionals and vice versa. It suggests that parks and recreation professionals can strengthen degree programs, accreditation, certification, and continuing education by incorporating specific youth development competencies established by the National Collaboration for Youth. For their part, youth development professionals can learn from parks and recreation professionals how to enhance recreation programming as part of their services by gaining an understanding of program design, program and activity leadership, and administrative practices. With much debate over whether more education or more experience is a better path for those working with youth, the authors suggest that a combination of both will adhere to the quality of staff. Staff gain further knowledge and skill from academic preparation at the undergraduate and graduate levels, field-based training through jobs and internships, and continuing education courses specializing in youth development competencies and recreation-based competencies set within a youth development environment.

NEW DIRECTIONS FOR YOUTH DEVELOPMENT • DOI: 10.1002/yd

Chapter Nine: Reframing recreation as a public policy priority

Phillip Lovell

Recreation has the potential to be an important public policy priority; however, it must be reframed to address critical policy priorities. Few policymakers understand the value and benefits of recreation, requiring practitioners and advocates to closely connect recreation to issues of concern to policymakers. A significant policy opportunity to expand recreational opportunities for children and youth lies in the area of education, including the reauthorization of the Elementary and Secondary Education Act. By educating policymakers on the myriad outcomes that can result from quality recreational experiences, including the ways in which recreation can support the education of children and youth, solid, incremental progress can be made in positioning recreation as a public policy priority.

NEW DIRECTIONS FOR YOUTH DEVELOPMENT • DOI: 10.1002/yd

*Personally meaningful and positive leisure pursuits
are powerful mechanisms for adolescent development. Elements and characteristics of leisure experiences contribute directly to the development of
identity, autonomy, competence, initiative, civic
duty, and social connections.*

1

Leisure, recreation, and play from a developmental context

Linda L. Caldwell, Peter A. Witt

THE TERMS *PLAY, RECREATION, AND LEISURE* can evoke thoughts of fri-
volity, fun, sociability, competition, slothfulness, or idleness. However, there is substantial evidence that what people do in their
discretionary or free time has important developmental and health
implications. Therefore, to introduce this special issue, this article
examines how play, recreation, and leisure contribute to adolescent
development and the conditions that facilitate that development.

A large proportion of a nonworking adolescent's day is considered "free time." By some estimates, this time fills about 40 percent of an adolescent's day.[1] The way in which an adolescent fills
this time has important developmental and health implications. Of
interest for this volume are the developmental benefits of filling
this time with positive experiences of play, recreation, and leisure.
Defining these terms depends on who is asked; complicating the
situation is that the terms are often used interchangeably. Leisure
scholars tend to consider leisure as the overall container for
positive experiences and may include activity-based pursuits, as

NEW DIRECTIONS FOR YOUTH DEVELOPMENT, NO. 130, SUMMER 2011 © WILEY PERIODICALS, INC.
Published online in Wiley Online Library (wileyonlinelibrary.com) • DOI: 10.1002/yd.394

well as the state of being reflective and experiencing freedom. For many adolescents, some portion of their leisure activities takes place during out-of-school-time programs, such as scouting, 4-H, youth sports, and community park and recreation programs; others play out in self-managed, family, or other nonstructured contexts.

Adolescents can also fill their free time in unhealthy or unproductive ways, such as being involved in vandalism or using alcohol or other drugs. Many adults consider these to be negative behaviors, even though some adolescents may consider these activities to be simply fun and recreational. Some researchers have suggested that these activities can also contribute to development and that they are part of growing up if they are experimental rather than addictive.[2] Often these types of activities are motivated when adolescents perceive they are bored in their free time and have nothing else to do.

In this article, we discuss positive developmental benefits associated with filling free time in positive ways. Although there are differences in the use of the terms *play, recreation, and leisure*, we will avoid the semantic quagmire and use the term *leisure* to convey the positive ways that adolescents can fill their free time. As we discuss these developmental outcomes, we describe in more detail the characteristics of leisure pursuits and experiences that contribute to these outcomes.

The examination of leisure pursuits from an activity, context, and experiential perspective in many ways differentiates the way leisure scientists study adolescent leisure from the way developmental psychologists study it (although there are exceptions). That is, leisure scientists tend to focus on the whole leisure experience, including activity and time use, context, and experience, such as the leisure activity, context, and experience model,[3] rather than taking a "time" or "activity" perspective that developmental psychologists typically, but not always, adopt. What has been missing in the field of leisure sciences is a more sophisticated examination of development using modern longitudinal analytical techniques such as latent transition analysis. We hope this article and this entire special issue contribute to further dialogue on the importance of leisure to adolescent development.

Plugged In: A case study

We begin our discussion with a recent story from the *Christian Science Monitor* about two parents who started a nonprofit organization, Plugged In (PI).[4] The mission of PI is to enable youth to have a positive effect on their world through music. The story of PI serves as a platform to begin a discussion of how leisure contributes to youth development.

PI began when Sandra Rizkallah and Tom Pugh heard their teenagers and their teenagers' friends talking about wanting to be in a rock and roll band. But nothing happened. Realizing that there were no places in the Boston area for these teens to get support for their dreams, they decided to help. Pugh had studied bass at the Berklee College of Music and played in bands as a professional musician. With his talents and his wife's vision, they started PI with five teens who participated in a course to learn to play in a rock band. Eight years later, more than four hundred teens have participated in the program. During three sixteen-week sessions every year, ninety-five teens play in twenty-eight bands and learn from area professionals in classes that have about four to six students per class.

The story of PI demonstrates that what youth do in their leisure time can make powerful contributions to human development and health. PI was developed to provide an avenue for adolescents to learn music and how to play in a rock band, but the fundamental vision was that music could be a vehicle for social change through helping others. Thus, at the beginning of each session, all participants attend a town hall meeting where they select a charity or cause to receive monies raised from their concerts and the sale of their CDs. They also sponsor a Jam-a-Thon fundraiser for the selected charity or cause. At the meeting, students pitch their ideas about which charity or cause to support. This process is entirely run by the teens.

NEW DIRECTIONS FOR YOUTH DEVELOPMENT • DOI: 10.1002/yd

The anecdotal story of PI's effectiveness is supportive of the substantial empirical evidence of the powerful developmental outcomes that are associated with positive leisure-time activities. Comments from the founders of the PI program and its students, counselors, and parents provide some insights into the impact of the program:[5]

Many teens come to us struggling with low self-esteem. Through connecting with other young musicians in Plugged In, they learn they can help others through their love of music. They gain confidence, compassion, a social conscience—and hope. We provide a safe place for these kids. They have so many pressures. . . . Here, kids can take risks, and they can be kind to each other. And that brings strength.
—One of the program founders

I learned to work in a group, and to share my opinions and ideas. And most of all, to never be afraid to try new things—even if you make a complete goof of yourself—and to be outspoken about what I believe in.
—College student who spent six years in the program

Plugged In is more than a music program. It's a place for youths to connect with one another in a noncompetitive way. That's why I love this program. If a young person isn't an athlete or part of a school-based group, there are virtually no places that offer an opportunity to grow and connect with their peers.
—Jon Mattleman, director of Needham Youth Services

It's been wonderful for him, especially in boosting his self-confidence. Plugged In has helped him improve as a musician, but it's also empowered him to see how he can use his music to make a difference in the world.
—Parent of son who has been playing bass guitar in the program for six years

Leisure and adolescent development

Developmental benefits occur in leisure for a variety of reasons. The PI story provides a number of lessons about how leisure pursuits can contribute to adolescent development. One of these lessons is the importance of having appropriate environmental supports and opportunities. For example, caring adults who respect adolescents' capabilities and provide a supportive push to learn skills and competencies are critical to the developmental process. Providing supports to help youth develop their own voices and make decisions can be powerful vehicles for development.

Larson and his colleagues have described youth experiences in both adult-led and youth-led endeavors and the complexities surrounding youth leadership and youth voice.[6] The most successful adult-youth partnerships occur when adults adopt a scaffolding model, providing the appropriate amount of support and the resources that adolescents need at each stage of their development to be successful.

A rich empirical literature documents the importance of how appropriate structure, organization, and leadership contribute to adolescent development. For example, research shows that adolescents who participate in structured extracurricular activities are less likely to engage in antisocial behavior, more likely to have a higher level of academic achievement, and more likely to have positive psychosocial functioning.[7]

Unstructured activities are often defined as being unsupervised or having no focus on skill building.[8] When defined as such, unsupervised activity participation typically is linked to negative outcomes. For example, hanging out has been positively related to alcohol initiation, and sedentary activities such as watching TV and playing video games are related to outcomes such as overweight and diminished physical activity among adolescents.[9]

Some researchers and theorists, however, have argued that unstructured time is important for healthy development and self-expression.[10] Elkins posits that many contemporary children and adolescents are overscheduled, making them more likely to be stressed and less likely to engage in important activities such as playing in a natural, creative way.[11] Furthermore, when unstructured activities are defined more broadly, research findings are more positive. For example, participation in activities like backpacking and chess has value for expressing and affirming identity among college students, and virtual online peer-to-peer interactions contribute to informal learning.[12]

What is often missing from the literature, however, is a deeper understanding of why leisure is an important context for adolescent development. These benefits can occur because leisure offers a number of conditions or characteristics associated with addressing developmental tasks of adolescents. These are described next.

Autonomy development and self-determination

One of the defining elements of leisure is that it is characterized by free choice and self-determination. That is, in leisure, adolescents make choices to engage in activities they enjoy and give them meaning. The feeling of freedom and choice in leisure facilitates being open to and gaining developmental benefits. As young people mature, developing behavioral and emotional autonomy is an important task. Leisure pursuits are ideal contexts for autonomy development given that they are characterized by self-determination. Adults who facilitate growth experiences through providing appropriate structure (or lack of structure) in leisure play a critical role in adolescent development through leisure. Conversely, leisure pursuits that are not self-determined tend to be experienced negatively and can quickly lead to cessation of participation.

Intrinsic and identified motivation, initiative, and goal setting

Autonomy development and self-determination are intricately linked with developing initiative and goal setting skills. Often leisure is considered an end, not a means to an end. That is, it is pursued for its own sake and thus is internally rewarding. For example, someone may love to run because it feels good. Although running may be a form of exercise and contribute to health, the primary motivation is running for its own sake. A great deal of research suggests that intrinsically motivated activities are related to health and well-being.[13] Leisure is an important context for intrinsic forms of motivation.

Leisure can also be a means to an end. Purposeful leisure (that is, doing a leisure activity to achieve a goal) is also beneficial if the goal is meaningful to and endorsed by the adolescent. In the PI case, playing in a rock band to raise money for a cause that is personally endorsed and part of one's value system is, in most cases, intrinsic in nature, even though it is goal oriented.

Leisure pursuits thus offer myriad opportunities for adolescents to experience doing an activity for internal rewards, as opposed to doing an activity out of external compulsion. Of course, there are many free-time activities that adolescents engage in due to some form of external compulsion. Peer pressure, parental demands, and external rewards such as trophies are all motivating. However, participation driven solely by external factors is unlikely to help adolescents reap important developmental and health benefits as much as internally motivated action.

Internally motivated pursuits are more likely to be sustained over time. Adolescents who are internally motivated are more likely to remain focused and stick to a personally desired activity even when they face challenges, such as transportation difficulties or lack of initial skill. Undertaking internally motivated leisure pursuits leads to the development of initiative, which is important to fostering the transition from adolescence to adulthood.[14] Furthermore, intrinsically motivated pursuits are more likely to be personally expressive and to reflect one's true self-identity.[15]

Achievement and competence

Perceived competence and a sense of achievement contribute to intrinsic motivation. Leisure pursuits are excellent mechanisms for developing skills and a sense of mastery. As illustrated in the PI example, leisure pursuits offer many avenues for developing skills and competencies. Youth engaged in learning how to play in a rock and roll band not only gained music skills, but also learned to work with others, take personal risks, and contribute to society through their passions.

Leisure can also be a significant context for achievement and developing perceived competence for those who may in other ways feel less competent in school-based activities. All students can find a leisure activity in which they can excel, even if they are not as successful with academic material.

In addition, leisure pursuits can contribute to educational attainment by influencing academic achievement at school and through informal learning that occurs outside the traditional classroom. For example, there is fairly consistent evidence that extracurricular activities are associated with educational success, even when controlling for academic ability, family background, and other extracurricular activities.[16] Youth whose leisure activities are characterized by participation in more organized or structured activities and fewer passive and unstructured activities have better academic performance compared to those with the opposite profile.[17]

A second, but often overlooked, avenue to increase educational attainment is through informal learning that takes place outside the classroom.[18] This type of learning is effective because most students are more engaged in leisure contexts than with typical academic classroom instruction. Having choices and being exposed to different opportunities is not only developmentally appropriate; it also stimulates passions and allows students to become intensely involved in a project.[19]

Identity

Leisure pursuits are an important avenue for adolescent identity formation. Pursuits that are internally motivated, self-determined, personally meaningful and expressive, and offer a chance to build competencies can become a way for adolescents to understand who they are in relation to others and the world around them. In the PI example, there is little doubt that the students who participated in the classes identified themselves as singers, songwriters, rock musicians, or some combination of these roles. Equally important, these youth no doubt saw themselves as part of a larger local and global community and recognized that they had an imperative to contribute to that society and found a means to do so.

Civic engagement, community connections, and developing a moral compass

As youth come to identify with a larger social context, they begin to develop a sense of community and undertake actions that can contribute to that community. As they mature, they also develop an understanding of social and cultural traditions and norms and a sense of right and wrong. For example, many adolescents form groups over the Internet around a common cause or use public spaces for marches or rallies to express their views. These leisure pursuits provide a means for them to explore their values and worldviews, gain civic skills, and connect to the larger community.[20] Involvement in these experiences is important to adolescents' transition to adulthood and contributes to their emerging identity as citizens.[21]

Social skills and social connections

Social activities are among the most commonly pursued forms of leisure among adolescents.[22] They are also the most commonly desired form of leisure because adolescents crave the feeling that they belong. The social context of leisure is important to adolescent development in that it provides opportunities to learn empathy, loyalty, and intimacy in group activities,[23] as well as to negotiate with peers, resolve conflict, and work together for communal goals. Developmentally, social leisure activities allow both differentiation and integration and facilitate youth's abilities to exert personal control over their environments.

Leisure is an important context in which adolescents can experience safe places to try out different roles and interact informally with members of the opposite sex, as well as develop and learn about dealing with romantic relationships. Leisure is a particularly important context during puberty.

Leisure pursuits can also provide opportunities for youth to develop social capital: the social, cultural, and material resources young people acquire to help them in the various contexts of their lives and in the transition to adulthood.[24] Social capital is likely to develop when youth work together for a common goal, whether it is a protest against some injustice, lobbying for a skate park or youth center, or other type of collective activity.

Where and when social interactions take place is also important. Many structured and unstructured leisure activities are sought out and provide opportunities for face-to-face social interaction. But youth also spend a great deal of time with social media and on the Internet. A 2009 study revealed that about 93 percent of U.S. teens used the Internet, spending about six and a half hours a day involved with some type of media.[25] Some research has suggested that use of media and technology is to blame for decreases in interpersonal skills, academic achievement, violence, and identity confusion and increased cyberbullying. However, other studies report that adolescents gain social skills, feelings of belonging, academic skills, leadership skills, and creativity through screen time and the use of media and technology.[26]

Emotional response to leisure

A final but essential consideration is that adolescents often report positive emotional experiences in leisure, which can serve as a relief from the stress they feel in other areas of their lives and contribute to positive psychological adjustment and well-being.[27] Joy, fun, excitement, interest, and happiness are hallmarks of leisure. In addition, leisure is a rich context to experience flow, a state of consciousness in which there is a "merging of action and awareness"[28] and time passes without thought. The happiest adolescents tend to be more often engaged in flow-producing situations.[29]

Of course, adolescents may also experience negative emotional experiences in their leisure. Stress and embarrassment, boredom, and loneliness can be associated with leisure pursuits. Adolescents can also feel pressure from their peers to engage in activities that they would not normally pursue.

The developing brain, social and emotional regulation, and risk and experimentation

Recent advances in understanding the developing brain are relevant to adolescent leisure. Between ages twelve and seventeen, the adolescent brain is easily shaped and thus receptive to the influence of social learning through interaction with adults and peers. During this time, the developing brain is primed for developing enduring interests. The amygdala, the brain's center for emotion and emotion-based memory, becomes particularly active during early adolescence. This early activation of emotions and passions intensifies goal-directed behavior and is often manifested by developing passions in music, art, recreational hobbies, and sports.[30] The activation of interests comes about because when certain connections among neurons are used, they are strengthened; those that are not used are pruned. Consequently adolescent brains are primed to become hardwired for developing leisure activity preferences, setting the stage for continued participation throughout adulthood.

Because of this brain activity, adolescence is also a time of increased sensation seeking and risk taking. Thus, adolescents have a natural tendency to seek out and participate in intense and exciting situations. Adolescents like novelty and have the capacity to deal with or gravitate to multiple forms of simultaneous stimuli.[31]

Executive functioning skills, such as good decision making, critical reflection, and problem solving, evolve a bit after the amygdala is activated. In part, this may account for why youth often make poor judgments in emotionally charged situations. For example, an intense emotional response to a situation may prevent an adolescent from correctly interpreting another's emotional state, and the brain is often unable to govern this emotional situation with a more neutral or clear-headed response.

Leisure pursuits provide excellent avenues for practicing social and emotional regulation due to the often intense emotional experiences that accompany such pursuits. Leisure pursuits are also excellent vehicles for youth to initiate and practice executive functioning skills. These processes are particularly true if there are adults who can help youth develop skills through debriefing activities and structuring situations. Moreover, providing safe risks through leisure activities is one way to help mitigate possible unfavorable outcomes (for example, personal injury or injury to others and vandalism) due to the need for behavioral risk and excitement.

Conclusion

Leisure and recreation contexts have the potential to be important contexts for adolescent development. Research that focuses on all aspects of leisure-time activities—activity and time use, context, and experience—across time promises to be a fertile ground for continued research in the importance of leisure to adolescent development.

Notes

1. Larson, R. W., & Verma, S. (1999). How children and adolescents spend time across the world: Work, play, and developmental opportunities. *Psychological Bulletin, 125*, 701–736.

2. Leather, N. C. (2009). Risk-taking behavior in adolescence: A literature review. *Journal of Child Health Care, 13*, 295–304.

3. Caldwell, L. L. (2005). Recreation and youth development. In P. Witt & L. Caldwell (Eds.), *Recreation and youth development* (pp. 169–189). State College, PA: Venture Publishing.

4. Jones, M. (2010, October). Helping teens be a real guitar hero—by caring for others. *Christian Science Monitor.* Retrieved from http://www.csmonitor.com/USA/Society/2010/1025/Helping-teens-be-a-real-guitar-hero-by-caring-for-others?sms_ss=twitter&at_xt=4cc649e259e4b35f,0.

5. Jones. (2010).

6. Dworkin, J. B., Larson, R., & Hansen, D. (2003). Adolescents' accounts of growth experiences in youth activities. *Journal of Youth and Adolescence, 32*, 17–26; Hansen, D. M., Larson, R. W., & Dworkin, J. B. (2003). What adolescents learn in organized youth activities: A survey of self-reported developmental experiences. *Journal of Research on Adolescence, 13*, 25–55.

7. Mahoney, J. L. (2000). Participation in school extracurricular activities as a moderator in the development of antisocial patterns. *Child Development, 71*, 502–516; Mahoney, J. L., & Stattin, H. (2000). Leisure activities and adolescent antisocial behavior: The role of structure and social context. *Journal*

of Adolescence, 23, 113–127; Zaff, J. F., Moore, K. A., Papillo, A. R., & Williams, S. (2003). Implications of extracurricular activity participation during adolescence on positive outcomes. *Journal of Adolescent Research, 18*(6), 599–630; Bartko, W. T., & Eccles, J. S. (2003). Adolescent participation in structured and unstructured activities: A person-oriented analysis. *Journal of Youth and Adolescence, 32*, 233–242; Mahoney, J. L., Cairns, B. D., & Farmer, T. W. (2003). Promoting interpersonal competence and educational success through extracurricular activity participation. *Journal of Educational Psychology, 95*, 409–418; Bartko, W. T., & Eccles, J. S. (2003). Adolescent participation in structured and unstructured activities: A person-oriented analysis. *Journal of Youth and Adolescence, 32*, 233–242.

   8. Mahoney, J. L., Harris, A. L., & Eccles, J. S. (2006). Organized activity participation, positive youth development, and the over-scheduled hypothesis. *Society for Research on Child Development: Social Policy Report: Giving Child and Youth Development Knowledge Away, 20*, 3–25; Osgood, D. W., Anderson, A. L., & Shaffer, J. N. (2005). Unstructured leisure in the after-school hours. In J. Mahoney, R. Larson, & J. Eccles (Eds.), *Organized activities as contexts of development: Extracurricular activities, after-school and community programs* (pp. 45–64). Mahwah, NJ: Erlbaum; Persson, A., Kerr, M., & Stattin, H. (2007). Staying in or moving away from structured activities: Explanation involving parents and peers. *Developmental Psychology, 43*, 197–207.

   9. Strycker, L. A., Duncan, S. C., & Pickering, M. A. (2003). The social context of alcohol initiation among African American and white youth. *Journal of Ethnicity in Substance Abuse, 2*, 35–42; Koezuka, N., Koo, M., Allison, K. R., Adlaf, E. M., Dwyer, J.J.M., Faulkner, G., & Goodman, J. (2006). The relationship between sedentary activities and physical inactivity among adolescents: Results from the Canadian Community Health Survey. *Journal of Adolescent Health, 39*, 515–522; Motl, R. W., McAuley, E., Birnbaum, A. S., & Lytle, L. A. (2006). Naturally occurring changes in time spent watching television are inversely related to frequency of physical activity during early adolescence. *Journal of Adolescence, 29*, 19–32.

   10. Kleiber, D. A. (1999). *Leisure experience and human development: A dialectical interpretation.* New York, NY: Basic Books.

   11. Elkins, D. (2003, January–February). The overbooked child: Are we pushing our kids too hard? *Psychology Today, 36*(1), 64–69. Retrieved from http://proquest.umi.com.ezproxy.librarieis.psu.edu.

   12. Haggard, L. M., & Williams, D. R. (1992). Identity affirmation through leisure activities: Leisure symbols of the self. *Journal of Leisure Research, 24*(1), 1–18; Horst, M. I., Bittanti, M., Boyd, D., Herr-Stephenson, B., Lange, P. G., Pascoe, C. J., Robinson, L., . . . Tripp, L. (2008). *Living and learning with new media: Summary of findings from the Digital Youth Project.* Chicago, IL: John D. and Catherine T. MacArthur Foundation. Retrieved from http://digitalyouth.ischool.berkeley.edu/files/report/digitalyouth-WhitePaper.pdf.

   13. Hunter, J. P., & Csikszentmihalyi, M. (2003). The positive psychology of interested adolescents. *Journal of Youth and Adolescence, 32*(1), 27–35; Larson, R. W. (2000). Toward a psychology of positive youth development. *American Psychologist, 55*, 170–183.

14. Larson, R. W. (2000). Toward a psychology of positive youth development. *American Psychologist, 55*, 170–183; Kleiber, D. A., Larson, R., & Csikszentmihalyi, M. (1986). The experience of leisure in adolescence. *Journal of Leisure Research, 18*(3), 169–176.

15. Waterman, A. S. (2004). Finding someone to be: Studies on the role of intrinsic motivation in identity formation. *Identity, 4*(3), 209–228.

16. Darling, N., Caldwell, L. L., & Smith, R. (2005). Participation in school-based extracurricular activities and adolescent adjustment. *Journal of Leisure Research, 37*, 51–77; Mahoney, J. L., Cairns, B. D., & Farmer, T. W. (2003). Promoting interpersonal competence and educational success through extracurricular activity participation. *Journal of Educational Psychology, 95*, 409–418; Camp, W. G. (1990). Participation in school activities and achievement: A covariance structural analysis. *Journal of Educational Research, 83*, 272–278.

17. Bartko, W. T., & Eccles, J. S. (2003). Adolescent participation in structured and unstructured activities: A person-oriented analysis. *Journal of Youth and Adolescence, 32*, 233–242.

18. Ferrandino, V. L. (2007). *A new day for learning.* Report from the Time, Learning and Afterschool Task Force, funded by C. S. Mott Foundation. Retrieved from http://www.edutopia.org/anewdayforlearning.

19. Chung, A., & Hillsman, E. (2005). Evaluating after-school programs. *The School Administrator.* Arlington, VA: American Association of School Administrators, Retrieved from http://archives.aasa.org/publications/saarticledetail.cfm?ItemNumber=2516&snItemNumber=&tnItemNumber= ; Dahl, R. (2004). Adolescent brain developoment: A period of vulnerabilities and opportunities. *Annals of New York Academies of Science, 1021*, 1–22.

20. Fredricks, J. A., & Eccles, J. S. (2005). Developmental benefits of extracurricular involvement: Do peer characteristics mediate the link between activities and youth outcomes? *Journal of Youth and Adolescence, 34*, 507–520; Larson, R. W. (2001). How U.S. children and adolescents spend time: What it does (and doesn't) tell us about their development. *Current Directions in Psychological Science, 10*, 160–164; Steinberg, L., & Morris, A. S. (2001). Adolescent development. *Annual Review of Psychology, 52*, 83–110.

21. Damon, W. (2001). To not fade away: Restoring civil identity among the young. In D. Ravitch & J. Viteritte (Eds.), *Making good citizens: Education and civil society.* New Haven, CT: Yale University Press; Flanagan, C. (2003). Developmental roots of political engagement. *Ps: Political Science and Politics, 36*, 257–261; Youniss, J., McLellan, J. A., & Yates, M. (1997). What we know about engendering civic identity. *American Behavioral Scientist, 40*, 620–631.

22. Kleiber, D. A., Caldwell, L. L., & Shaw, S. A. (1993). Leisure meanings among adolescents, *Loisir et Société/Leisure and Society, 16*, 99–114.

23. Dworkin et al. (2003).

24. Holland, J., Reynolds, T., & Weller, S. (2007). Transitions, networks and communities: The significance of social capital in the lives of children and young people. *Journal of Youth Studies, 10*, 97–116; Weller, S. (2006). Skateboarding alone? Making social capital discourse relevant to teenagers' lives.

Journal of Youth Studies, 9, 557–574. doi:10.1080/13676260600805705. http://dx.doi.org/10.1080/13676260600805705.

25. Roberts, D. F., Foehr, U. G., & Rideout, V. (2005). *Generation M: Media in the lives of 8–18 year olds.* Menlo Park, CA: Kaiser Family Foundation.

26. Greenhow, C., & Robelia, B. Informal learning and identity formation in online social networks. *Learning, Media and Technology, 34,* 119–140.

27. Dworkin et al. (2003).

28. Csikszentmihalyi, M., & Kleiber, D. A. (1999). Leisure and self-actualization. In B. L. Driver, P. J. Brown, & G. L. Peterson (Eds.), *Benefits of leisure* (pp. 91–102). State College, PA: Venture Publishing (p. 95).

29. Csikszentmihalyi, M., & Hunter, J. (2003). Happiness in everyday life: The uses of experience sampling. *Journal of Happiness Studies, 4*(2), 185–199.

30. Giedd, J., Blumenthal, J., Jeffries, N., Castellanos, F., Liu, H., Zijdenbos, A., Paus, T., . . . Rapoport, J. (1999). Brain development during childhood and adolescence: A longitudinal MRI study. *Nature Neuroscience, 2,* 861–863; Dahl, R. (2004). Adolescent brain development: A period of vulnerabilities and opportunities. *Annals of New York Academies of Science, 1021,* 1–22.

31. Dahl. (2004).

LINDA L. CALDWELL *is professor of recreation, park and tourism management and human development and family studies at the Pennsylvania State University.*

PETER A. WITT holds *the Bradberry Recreation and Youth Development Chair at Texas A&M University.*

Family leisure involvement may provide the first and most essential context for positive youth development in today's society.

2

Positive youth development within a family leisure context: Youth perspectives of family outcomes

Peter J. Ward, Ramon B. Zabriskie

STRUCTURED AND ORGANIZED PROGRAMS and activities provide valuable settings for youth development. However, the primary setting of the home should be considered the first, and perhaps the most essential, context for positive youth development. Within the home environment, the parents are often the most invested adults in the lives of youth. Parental involvement is one of the strongest protective factors an adolescent can have related to maximizing his or her potential.[1] Evidence supports that strong, positive parental influence contributes to preventing adolescent risky behaviors such as drug and alcohol use and promiscuity.[2] Positive interaction within the family clearly provides the context that has the potential to play the most significant role when considering experiences that can foster meaningful relationships, help develop skills and competencies, and influence all aspects of a youth's environment. When considering family life, Zabriskie and McCormick stated, "Besides family crisis, shared leisure may be one of the few experiences that bring family members together for any significant amount of time today."[3]

NEW DIRECTIONS FOR YOUTH DEVELOPMENT, NO. 130, SUMMER 2011 © WILEY PERIODICALS, INC.
Published online in Wiley Online Library (wileyonlinelibrary.com) • DOI: 10.1002/yd.395

Scholars have long reported that family leisure involvement serves a purposive role that fosters specific individual and family outcomes. Shaw and Dawson reported that parents "consciously and deliberately" plan and facilitate family leisure activities in order to achieve particular short- and long-term goals: improving family relationships; enhancing family communication; promoting skills, health, fitness, and sportsmanship; teaching moral lessons; instilling values; and creating family unity and identity.[4] Parents reported that family leisure was so integral to healthy family life that it was with a "sense of urgency" they planned to spend time with children participating in family activities. Mactavish and Schleien reported similar findings in that families viewed family leisure primarily as a means to promote overall quality of family life—for example, family unity, satisfaction, and physical and mental health—and for helping family members learn values and develop life skills, including social skills such as problem solving, compromising, and negotiation.[5]

Harrington also identified the intentional nature of family leisure in which parents organize activities in an effort to build and strengthen family relationships through togetherness and child socialization.[6] She reported on the critical nature of family leisure as a context in which essential parenting, interaction, and bonding occur, particularly between fathers and their children. For example, she found that children's sport does more than provide a vital environment in which fathers can share common interests and bond during common experiences; it also "provides concrete ways of supporting children in their activities and occasions for private and meaningful conversations."[7] In other words, it appears that parents, as invested adults, purposively or intentionally plan family leisure experiences to create and maintain meaningful relationships and provide supportive opportunities for their children to learn skills and develop behaviors that will both strengthen family life and contribute to their overall positive development. Such conclusions sound strikingly similar to the definition of positive youth development. It is quite possible that family leisure involvement may provide the first and most essential context for positive youth development in society today.

Family systems framework

Similar to the broader ecological perspective used in the youth development literature, family systems theory suggests that each individual in the family influences the whole, while the whole family also influences each individual.[8] In other words, the whole is greater than the sum of its parts. Zabriskie and McCormick summarized family systems theory by stating that it "holds that families are goal directed, self correcting, interconnected systems that both affect and are affected by their environment and by qualities within the family system itself."[9] Therefore, from a systems perspective, examination of family variables is likely to provide valuable insight into both family and individual outcomes. This logic suggests it may be useful to examine family leisure and related family outcomes particularly from the perspective of an adolescent family member. Such an approach provides valuable insight and direction when considering family leisure as a context for positive youth development.

Core and balance model of family leisure

Researchers have reported significant relationships between family leisure involvement and positive family outcomes for over seven decades.[10] One theoretical model that has been established as a useful framework to examine family leisure in recent years is the core and balance model of family leisure functioning.[11] The model, grounded in family systems theory, indicates that involvement in different patterns of family leisure contributes to family functioning in different ways. Iso-Ahola indicated that individuals have a tendency to look for stability and change, structure and variety, and familiarity and novelty in their leisure.[12] That is, they tend to meet needs for both stability and change through their leisure behavior. Freeman and Zabriskie explained that this interplay and balance between stability and change plays a much greater role when considering the needs of a family as a whole.[13] They clarified that the balance of these needs is an underlying concept of family systems theory indicating that families continually seek a dynamic state of homeostasis. In other words, families must meet both the need for stability in interactions, structure, and relationships and the need for novelty in experience, input, and challenge in order to function and develop effectively.[14]

The core and balance model identifies two basic categories or patterns of family leisure, core and balance, that families use to meet needs for both stability and change, and ultimately facilitate outcomes of family cohesion and adaptability which are primary components of family functioning (see Figure 2.1). Core family leisure includes "common, everyday, low-cost, relatively accessible, often home-based activities that many families do frequently."[15] This may include family activities such as playing board games together, making and eating dinner together, watching movies or television together in the home, playing in the yard, gardening together, shooting hoops in the driveway, or simply jumping in the pile of leaves once the raking is done. Such activities often require minimal planning and resources; are quite spontaneous or informal; provide a safe, consistent, and typically positive context in which family relationships tend to be enriched; and increase feelings of family closeness.

Balance family leisure is "depicted by activities that are generally less common, less frequent, more out of the ordinary, and usually not home-based thus providing novel experiences."[16] This may include family activities such as vacations, camping, fishing, special events, and trips to sporting events or theme parks. Such activities often require more investment of resources such as planning, time, effort, or money, and are therefore less spontaneous and more formalized. They tend to be more out of the ordinary and "include elements of unpredictability or novelty, which require family members to negotiate and adapt to new input and

Figure 2.1. Core and balance model of family leisure functioning

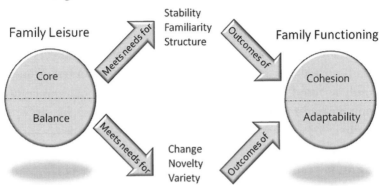

experiences that stand apart from everyday life."[17] They expose family members to unfamiliar stimuli from the environment and new challenges within a leisure context requiring them to learn, adapt, develop, and progress as a family unit.

Overall, the model suggests that core family leisure primarily meets family needs for familiarity and stability and tends to facilitate feelings of closeness, personal relatedness, family identity, bonding, and cohesion. Balance family leisure primarily meets family needs for novelty and change by providing the input necessary for families to be challenged, to develop, to adapt, and to progress as a working unit, and it helps foster the adaptive skills necessary to navigate the challenges of family life in today's society. Family systems theory holds that these two constructs, family cohesion and family adaptability, are necessary and are the primary components of healthy family functioning and wellness.[18] Similarly, findings related to the core and balance model suggest that involvement in both categories of family leisure is essential and that families who regularly participate in core and balance types of family leisure report higher levels of family functioning than those who participate in high or low amounts of either category.[19] Families who primarily participate in one category without the other are likely to experience disarray, frustration, and dysfunction.

Over the past decade, the core and balance model has provided a useful theoretical framework for examining family leisure among diverse family samples. Findings have provided considerable insight into the relationship of family leisure and family cohesion, family adaptability, and overall family functioning. Scholars have also reported consistent findings regarding the contribution of family leisure to a variety of related constructs, including family communication, family leisure satisfaction, and satisfaction with family life,[20] and have done so from different perspectives within the family of parents, young adults, and adolescents.

Findings among samples of large families have consistently reported that participation in both core and balance family leisure is essential, and from parents' perspectives in particular, both core and balance family leisure involvement have been equally significant in predicting family cohesion, adaptability, and overall family functioning.[21] Similar findings have also been reported when examining parent perspectives of other related variables. Zabriskie and McCormick found that for parents, both core and balance family leisure patterns contributed relatively equally to the explanation of satisfaction with family life.[22] They concluded that parents are likely to take a broader or more holistic perspective regarding their family's overall needs and development and appeared to do the same in their family leisure involvement. Parents reported both core and balance patterns, which are related to perceptions of both family cohesion and adaptability, contributed equally to family satisfaction. Zabriskie and McCormick's findings, however, also supported previous studies that have consistently reported the nature of the family leisure and family wellness relationship to be quite different from youth perspectives.

Youth perspectives of family leisure outcomes

When considering family leisure from a youth perspective, the core and balance model again provides a useful framework. Consider asking typical eleven- to fifteen-year-olds about their family leisure preferences or what types of family leisure activities they think are the most important for their family to participate in. Although one might think that typical adolescents would place much higher value on the new, exciting, more expensive, more challenging balance types of family activities such as vacations, camping, skiing, boating, and entertainment, studies have consistently found just the opposite. Responses from youth perspectives "have consistently reported core family leisure involvement to be a greater contributor to the explanation of family functioning than balance family leisure involvement in a variety of family samples."[23] In other words, "when all other factors are taken into account, youth in most families consider core family leisure involvement to play a particularly valuable role in relation to their evaluation of family functioning."[24] Freeman and Zabriskie found that from a youth perspective, core family leisure involvement was the only significant multivariate predictor of family functioning even though both core and balance had significant univariate relationships.[25] They concluded that families in their sample, particularly the youth, indicated that "regular involvement in common everyday, low-cost, relatively accessible, and often home-based activities with family members was the best predictor of aspects of family functioning such as emotional closeness, feelings of connectedness, mutual respect and a family system's ability to be flexible in roles, rules, and relationships." They also explained that although core family leisure appeared to play a particularly meaningful role related to family functioning, due to the interrelationship between core and balance family leisure, balance types of family activities should not be abandoned. While examining the role of family leisure in facilitating improved family communication from a youth perspective, Smith, Freeman, and Zabriskie[26] also found that core family leisure had a stronger relationship to family functioning than balance and supported Freeman and Zabriskie's[27] claim that core family leisure involvement was "essential to higher family functioning and may make a more valuable contribution to family life." They concluded that "core family leisure in particular offers parents an unobtrusive, enjoyable venue in which family members can interact frequently for small periods of time in or around the home. Thus, under the guise of family fun, families can take small steps toward better communication and more functional interaction."[28]

Similar findings have also been reported when examining other related family variables. Zabriskie and McCormick found that core family leisure involvement was the only factor that had a significant positive correlation to the youth's perception of family satisfaction from a multivariate level. They suggested the "fact that the core patterns stood out among the youth may be related to their need for consistency and stability in family activity patterns particularly during early adolescent development." In examining the differences in parent and youth responses, they found parents were more satisfied with their family life when they were involved in family leisure that was new and challenging, thus addressing the family's need for change and facilitating the teaching and learning of better adaptive skills and abilities. The youth, in contrast, appeared to have greater need for stability, consistency, and regularity in their preferences for family leisure. Therefore, they concluded, "While parents may have a greater need to teach new skills and prepare the family for the future with leisure, their children may simply desire to attain a stable sense of belongingness and closeness through family leisure."[29]

Other studies have found similar results when examining the quality of family leisure involvement. Agate, Zabriskie, Agate, and Poff reported that among their large national sample of families, "core family leisure satisfaction was the single greatest predictor of satisfaction with family life and explained up to twice as much variance as balance family leisure satisfaction" not only from a youth perspective, but from a parent and family perspective as well. They again recognized that satisfaction with balance family leisure involvement was still a significant factor and should not be discounted since involvement and satisfaction with both categories were likely to complement one another and be most beneficial for families, as the model suggests. The authors concluded that findings from their sample were "quite clear, however, particularly from a youth perspective, that family involvement and satisfaction with frequent, simple, home-based activities such as reading together, eating dinners together, playing board games, playing catch in the yard, and attending family members' games and performances, is absolutely essential to satisfaction with family life."[30]

Studies among different types of families are also consistent in their findings. In fact, among a sample of single-parent families, core family leisure involvement explained more variance in each aspect of family functioning than any other variable from not only the perspective of youth but from the parent and family perspective as well.[31] Authors have suggested that perhaps the necessity of essential core family leisure was more apparent among families that face greater stress, constraint, and difficulty by nature of their family structure, such as those with a child with a disability or single-parent families. Hornberger, Zabriskie, and Freeman concluded, "The need for consistent time together participating in regular home-based core family activities . . . appears to be more crucial when considering family functioning in single-parent households." In their qualitative inquiry into family resiliency following divorce, Hutchinson, Afifi, and Krause came to similar conclusions when they found everyday core types of family activities such as eating dinner, playing games, and simply being in the same room watching TV or visiting were overwhelmingly described as the most important activities done together by both the youth and parents in the single-parent families they studied.[32]

This finding regarding the involvement in and satisfaction with regular core types of family leisure and their relationship with positive family outcomes, particularly from a youth perspective, is so prevalent that it is difficult to find a family leisure study in the past decade that has not identified it. In fact, findings are also consistent among youth respondents in large, nationally reflective samples of families in other countries, including Australia ($N = 849$), New Zealand ($N = 371$), the United Kingdom ($N = 786$), and Canada ($N = 974$). Overall, the fact that youth clearly value regular, everyday, home-based, core types of family leisure involvement as it relates to positive family outcomes such as family functioning, family communication, and satisfaction with family life has obvious implications when considering positive youth development within a family leisure context.

Implications for families and youth programs

Adolescent development practitioners have typically considered programmed activities and environments as its primary tools in developing youth. The family context has nearly been excluded from the youth development arena. Among some possible reasons for excluding this context may be that some perceive many parents are unable to provide the types of activities that are widely believed to contribute to adolescent development, families lack the time and resources necessary to devote toward building adolescents, or parents do not know what activities will contribute to adolescent development. This line of logic of excluding the family, however, is not congruent with the fundamental definitions and principles of adolescent development.

One of the key factors for adolescent development is the interaction of invested adults in a consistent environment over a significant period of time. Parents could arguably be considered the most invested adults that adolescents encounter in their lives. Parents typically have and continue to build meaningful relationships with their children. The family environment serves as a laboratory where adolescents learn and develop skills, abilities, and competencies. Furthermore, families function as a community in which all family members, including adolescents, contribute to its success or failure. Thus, the family environment must be included in the youth development equation, possibly as the most influential contributor.

Within the family environment, not all types of activities are viewed as equal contributors to adolescent development. Adolescents report that core activities have a greater impact on their family functioning, family satisfaction, and family leisure satisfaction. Adolescents who are involved in core activities with their families are likely to be better prepared to develop into successful adults. This is contrary to what many parents would instinctively predict. Parents, similar to much of the adolescent development literature and practice, tend to participate in balance types of family activities with the vision that a few very significant experiences will have a meaningful and lasting impact on their youth. Furthermore, parents may envision adolescents as capable of drawing on the few meaningful balance experiences to create transformation within youth that will contribute to their development into healthy adults. Parents are not the only ones who hold these types of visions; many of the programs within adolescent development are also based on programming for the significant balance event that will have a meaningful impact on the development of an adolescent.

While balance events are important in adolescents' lives, according to family leisure research, core family leisure activities are also essential and may indeed be the most significant contributors to positive youth development. Therefore, we and others recommend that the common approaches to positive youth development such as outdoor adventure programs, after-school programs, community programs, and family camp programs consider the family and its possible influence on family life. They should also consider including core types of leisure programming. For example, community sports programmers can train volunteer coaches to encourage and require youth to practice regularly with family members. Rewards can be given as youth complete this homework assignment and thus foster regular home-based (core) family activities. Another example may be holding family game night where families come together as a unit and learn how to play board or card games. This could take place during the evening at a family camp or the community recreation center. During these structured activities, programmers can encourage families to continue the enjoyment of family game night as a regular home activity. Such examples are quite simple yet may have a profound impact in helping families to build core family leisure activities into part of their routines.

It is possible that families participating in such programs may be limited in basic essential skills for core family leisure such as simply playing a game together, necessitating the need for programmers to model and facilitate family core activities. Sometimes multiple programmed sessions may be required before families can participate in self-guided core activities in the home. By considering some family programming as well as how their programs can promote increased youth participation in core types of family leisure within the home, youth development programs are not only likely to become more successful but will have a significant impact on the first, and perhaps most essential, context for positive youth development: the family.

Notes

1. Witt, P., & Caldwell, L. (2005). *Recreation and youth development.* State College, PA: Venture.

2. Bahr, S. J., & Hoffman, J. P. (2010). Parenting style, religiosity, peers, and adolescent heavy drinking. *Journal of Studies on Alcohol and Drugs, 71*(4), 539–543.

3. Zabriskie, R., & McCormick, B. (2001). The influences of family leisure patterns on perceptions of family functioning. *Family Relations: Interdisciplinary Journal of Applied Family Studies, 50*(3), 281–289. P. 287.

4. Shaw, S., & Dawson, D. (2001). Purposive leisure: Examining parental discourses on family activities. *Leisure Sciences, 23,* 217–231.

5. Mactavish, J., & Schleien, S. (1998). Playing together growing together: Parents' perspectives on the benefits of family recreation in families that include children with a developmental disability. *Therapeutic Recreation Journal, 32*(3), 207–230.

6. Harrington, M. (2005). Family leisure and parents' subjective identities: Gendered ways of being a "good parent." In T. Delamere, C. Randall, & D. Robinson (Eds.), *Abstracts of papers presented at the Eleventh Canadian Congress on Leisure Research, May 17–20* (pp. 233–236). Waterloo: Canadian Association for Leisure Studies.

7. Harrington, M. (2006). Sport and leisure as contexts for fathering in Australian families. *Leisure Studies, 25*(2), 165–183. P. 177.

8. White, S. M., & Klein, D. M. (2008). *Family theories* (3rd ed.). Thousand Oaks, CA: Sage.

9. Zabriskie & McCormick (2001). P. 281.

10. Holman, T., & Epperson, A. (1989). Family leisure: A review of the literature with research recommendations. *Journal of Leisure Research, 16,* 277–294; Orthner, D., & Mancini, J. (1991). Benefits of leisure for family bonding. In B. L. Driver, P. J. Brown, & G. I. Peterson (Eds.), *Benefits of leisure* (pp. 215–301). State College, PA: Venture.

11. Zabriskie & McCormick. (2001).

12. Iso-Ahola, A. (1984). Social psychological foundations of leisure and resultant implications for leisure counseling. In E. T. Dowd (Ed.), *Leisure counseling: Concepts and applications* (pp. 97–125). Springfield, IL: Charles C. Thomas.

13. Freeman, P., & Zabriskie, R. (2003). Leisure and family functioning in adoptive families: Implications for therapeutic recreation. *Therapeutic Recreation Journal*, *37*(1), 73–93.

14. Klein, D., & White, J. (1996). *Family theories: An introduction.* Thousand Oaks, CA: Sage.

15. Zabriskie, R., & McCormick, B. (2003). Parent and child perspectives of family leisure involvement and satisfaction with family life. *Journal of Leisure Research*, *35*(2), 163–189.

16. Zabriskie & McCormick. (2003). P. 168.

17. Freeman & Zabriskie. (2003). P. 77.

18. Olson, D. (1986). Circumplex model VII: Validation studies and FACES II. *Family Process*, *25*, 337–351.

19. Freeman & Zabriskie. (2003); Zabriskie, & McCormick. (2001).

20. Smith, K., Freeman, P., & Zabriskie, R. (2009). An examination of family communication within the core and balance model of family leisure functioning. *Family Relations*, *58*, 79–90; Agate, J., Zabriskie, R., Agate, S., & Poff, R. (2009). Family leisure satisfaction and satisfaction with family life. *Journal of Leisure Research*, *41*(2), 205–223; Johnson, H., Zabriskie, R., & Hill, B. (2006). The contribution of couple leisure involvement, leisure time, and leisure satisfaction to marital satisfaction. *Marriage and Family Review*, *40*(1), 69–91; Poff, R., Zabriskie, R., & Townsend, J. (2010). Australian family leisure: Modeling parent and youth data. *Annals of Leisure Research*, *13*(3), 420–438; Zabriskie, R., & McCormick, B. (2003). Parent and child perspectives of family leisure involvement and satisfaction with family life. *Journal of Leisure Research*, *35*(2), 163–189.

21. Freeman & Zabriskie. (2003); Zabriskie & McCormick. (2001).

22. Zabriskie & McCormick. (2003).

23. Christenson, O., Zabriskie, R., Eggett, D., & Freeman, P. (2006). Family acculturation, family leisure involvement, and family functioning among Mexican-Americans. *Journal of Leisure Research*, *38*(4), 475–495; Dodd, D., Zabriskie, R., Widmer, M., & Eggett, D. (2009). Contributions of family leisure to family functioning among families that include children with developmental disabilities. *Journal of Leisure Research*, *41*(2), 261–286; Freeman & Zabriskie. (2003); Smith, K., Taylor, S., Hill, B., & Zabriskie, R. (2004). Family functioning and leisure in single parent families. *Abstracts from the 2004 Symposium on Leisure Research*, *53*. Ashburn, VA; National Recreation and Park Association; Zabriskie, R. B. (2000). *An examination of family and leisure behavior among families with middle school aged children* (Unpublished doctoral dissertation). Indiana University, Bloomington, Indiana.

24. Widmer, M., Zabriskie, R., & Loser, R. (2005). Wholesome family recreation. In S. R. Klein & E. J. Hill (Eds.), *Creating home as a sacred center:*

Principles for everyday living (pp. 205–215). Provo, UT: BYU Academic Publishing. P. 209.

25. Freeman & Zabriskie. (2003). P. 89.

26. Smith et al. (2009).

27. Freeman & Zabriskie. (2003). P. 90.

28. Smith et al. (2009). P. 88.

29. Zabriskie & McCormick. (2003). Pp. 180, 182.

30. Agate et al. (2009). P. 219.

31. Hornberger, L., Zabriskie, R., & Freeman, P. (2010). Contributions of family leisure to family functioning among single-parent families. *Leisure Sciences, 32*(2), 143–161. P. 153.

32. Hutchinson, S., Afifi, T., & Krause, S. (2007). The family that plays together fares better: Examining the contribution of shared family time to family resiliency following divorce. *Journal of Divorce & Remarriage, 46*(3/4), 21–48.

PETER J. WARD *is an assistant professor at Brigham Young University in the Department of Recreation Management and Youth Leadership.*

RAMON B. ZABRISKIE *is a professor at Brigham Young University in the Department of Recreation Management and Youth Leadership.*

This article describes a developmental series of coordinated stages that can enhance youth development through the integration of recreation and education activities.

3

Back to the future: The potential relationship between leisure and education

David S. Fleming, Lawrence R. Allen, Robert J. Barcelona

> Education has no more serious responsibility than making adequate provision for enjoyment of recreative leisure; not only for the sake of immediate health, but . . . for the sake of its lasting effect upon habits of mind.
>
> John Dewey (1916)

LEISURE AND EDUCATION HAVE been inextricably linked since the beginning of Greek civilization. However, the current view of and relationship among these notions has changed dramatically. The personnel, standards, vocational preparation, and contexts for each are largely separated. Within schools, there is little doubt that the era of No Child Left Behind has prompted a heightened focus on accountability for the academic outcomes that they produce. The recent economic downturn that has led to cuts in state and local budgets has exacerbated this result. Institutions and systems

NEW DIRECTIONS FOR YOUTH DEVELOPMENT, NO. 130, SUMMER 2011 © WILEY PERIODICALS, INC.
Published online in Wiley Online Library (wileyonlinelibrary.com) • DOI: 10.1002/yd.396

are focusing more heavily on their core missions and are downsizing or even eliminating services that are seen as noncentral or potentially harmful to the core. For schools, this has often meant that any programs that are not relevant to academic achievement are vulnerable in a time of fiscal uncertainty and political angst.

This perspective, pragmatic given the current economic and political conditions facing many communities, nevertheless bifurcates the natural and historical alignments that exist between leisure and education and quite possibly undermines the effectiveness of each. Given their central place in community life and the resources that they possess, schools serve as a natural and logical nexus for community building and development, beyond the basics of providing instruction in reading, writing, and math.

This community-focused approach has been embedded in a number of initiatives, including 21st Century Community Learning Centers initiatives and community schools movements. Yet while current economic conditions are threatening movements to integrate learning and development experiences, we argue for the need to continue to coordinate the efforts of both leisure services and education so that each might be more effective in achieving its mission. In this article, we draw a contemporary connection to the foundational and historical premises regarding leisure and education and suggest that an "education for leisure" perspective can be a productive orientation toward reaching the goals for each entity.

Leisure and education: The connection

The concept of leisure was introduced by the Greeks; their term for it, *schole*, is the root word for our *school*. The Greek concept of education recognized the important connection among the body, mind, and spirit. Meaningful leisure experiences were seen as both individual and societal goods that, when perfectly realized, could benefit both the person and the state. The Greeks therefore considered leisure as a worthy pursuit.

Of course, the popular interpretation of leisure today is far different from the Greek intention. Leisure was once seen as a way of life where one was free from obligation, and thereby allowed engagement in the highest forms of learning: music, poetry, literature, physical activity, and other forms of social discourse. Aristotle submitted that this classical view of leisure was considered the highest form of life and necessary to achieve excellence. Play also was a concept that the Greeks acknowledged, and Plato viewed it as the basis of education for children.

Although there are many concepts of leisure, the most popular definition today maintains the Greek concept of freedom from obligation and is viewed as a period of unobligated time, or free time. And, as John Dewey conveyed in *Democracy and Education* (1916), education has no greater responsibility than to prepare us for the recreative use of leisure.[1] By *recreative*, he was referring to restoring energy or revitalizing the body and spirit. Thus, leisure was viewed as a vehicle or medium for achieving or developing some personal or public good. But Dewey also was an advocate of educating people for life and therefore saw the value of leisure in terms of preparing people for a balanced lifestyle, which was important for well-being and happiness. He also endorsed play as a critical aspect of education.

In 1918, the federal Bureau of Education issued the Seven Cardinal Principles of Secondary Education:[2]

1. Health—providing health instruction, encouraging good health behavior and habits, providing opportunities to practice healthy living
2. Command of fundamental processes—development of the basic skills of writing, reading, oral and written expression, and math
3. Worthy home membership—development of those skills and qualities that make the individual a positive member of a family or group

4. Vocation—gaining an understanding of one's self and one's skills as they relate to potential work and career options
5. Civic education—development of an awareness and commitment to one's community, establishing a sense of civic responsibility and democratic ideals
6. Worthy use of leisure—provide the skills and develop the attitude to enrich one's body, mind, and spirit in their leisure
7. Ethical character—instilling an understanding and a sense of personal and social responsibility developing the principles of ethical behavior and decision making

These principles grew out of several decades of debate over the need for school reform in response to changing social environments and circumstances surrounding the beginning of the twentieth century. It can be argued that we are in a similar situation today at the beginning of the twenty-first century.

These broad-based goals speak to the integration of healthy leisure pursuits, beyond-the-classroom experiences, and the formal education curriculum. Yet today, many of these goals, particularly as they are tied to the school, are threatened. Certainly the sixth principle, the worthy use of leisure, has all but been forgotten. However, the social and health issues now facing our society underscore Dewey's points regarding the importance of the wise use of leisure. Thus, there is a strong historical linkage of leisure, recreation, and play with education.

Today the role of leisure in education varies considerably. Although there is a continuing voice for educating students for the worthy use of leisure, both as an end in itself and for achieving a balanced lifestyle, the more popular role is an instrumental one where leisure, recreation, and play are seen as avenues to address students' social or health issues. For example, because of the concern over childhood obesity, we have recently seen a resurgence of the importance of lifelong physical activity; thus, physical education is being expanded in many states, and many before- and after-school programs have a physical recreation component to supplement the formal physical education experiences of the students. These efforts are important, but they are not meeting their potential because there is often little to no coordination between in-school and out-of-school student experiences.

This potential linkage between leisure and education is also readily apparent in traditional subject areas such as art, music, dance, drama, literature, and science, as well as in basic skills such as reading and mathematics. The value is in the coordination and dialogue among educators and the professional providers of leisure services in these same areas. It can be argued that many leisure experiences have the potential for educational value. For example, if a class of students visits a museum, are they having an educational experience, a leisure experience, or both? Certainly the response depends on one's interpretation of the essential characteristics of a leisure experience. However, this experience clearly has the potential to be both, and providing complementary and purposeful leisure experiences can strengthen and positively reinforce their academic value.

One essential characteristic of leisure is a positive psychological response to the experience. For example, many museum curators develop engaging displays and interactive experiences to elicit a positive psychological response from the students. Their goal is to motivate students to seek further experiences at the museum. Certainly they would like the students to leave with an increased knowledge of the artifacts and historical events being presented. However, they are just as interested in developing a positive response to visiting a museum with the hope of encouraging future visits. This is where leisure and education are inextricably tied together—when students freely choose an educative experience such as visiting a museum, reading a book, engaging in healthy behaviors, or doing a science activity outside the school day. It is from this perspective that we offer the following ideas and thoughts regarding the educational role of leisure within youth development.

Coordinated stages

The value of an educational or leisure experience can be compounded when the two are coordinated. A museum experience that educates the child while also inducing an affective response resulting in a desire to return to the environment may have the greatest impact. The fields of leisure and education need not be separate entities (as they are often compartmentalized within a child's day). Rather, a coordinated experience among available resources and entities that share similar goals can help attain those goals in a more efficient and effective manner. Darling-Hammond has suggested that before-school, after-school, and even Saturday activities can be instrumental, especially if those opportunities are perceived as privileges.[3] However, the level of coordination can dictate the level of potential for enhancing this affective response. In this section, we describe a developmental series of coordinated stages (shared spaces, congruent programming, infusion, and integration) that can enhance youth development using the school as the nexus for these activities. These levels are somewhat hierarchical in nature, and programs should evaluate their own structure and strive to move toward higher levels of coordination.

Shared spaces

As an initial framework, the shared-spaces stage encourages the school and the community to share facilities for common

Table 3.1. Stages of coordination

Levels of coordination	Evidence	Student outcomes
Stage 4: Integration	Education for leisure	Youth demonstrate free choice to participate in learning and development activities
Stage 3: Infusion	Coordinated themes	Youth make connections among themes and constructs
Stage 2: Congruent programming	Coordinated schedules	Youth make connections among skills and activities
Stage 1: Shared spaces	Joint-use agreements	Youth participate in activities with ample resources

purposes. School facilities (elementary, middle, or secondary) often include field space, gym or other multipurpose space, classrooms, and even auditoriums. However, the normal school day usually ends between 2:00 and 4:00, so many of these spaces remain unoccupied or at best underused.[4]

The shared-spaces stage encourages a school to partner with local entities to share spaces beyond the school day while also encouraging partnerships in outcomes. Shared spaces require active support from the local school district, administrators, and teachers, as well as the support from the partnering agency. For example, a recreation department that uses a school gym for practice and competitions must schedule the use of the space to avoid conflicts. The shared-space stage constitutes a low level of coordination, yet it still requires specific efforts from the individuals involved. School officials who do not recognize these connections may be reticent to share facilities for upkeep or liability issues. As a response, joint-use agreements have been found to facilitate partnerships by establishing boundaries and encouraging collaboration.[5] Community resources that do not embrace these connections may not take adequate care of the space or the relationships among those who provide them.

Programs should not strive to accomplish shared spaces as an outcome. Rather, this should be perceived as an initial step toward coordinating an experience that connects the academic experiences within school and the opportunities for self-selecting activities beyond the school day. Sharing facilities and resources will not inherently construct this linkage, so programs that accomplish this first level of coordinated effort should plan to move those collaborations forward.

Congruent programming

Organizations and schools have reached a higher level of coordination when they embark on congruent programming. The purpose of this stage is to coordinate educational experiences so that there is overlap in delivery. Youth are able to develop meaning and make connections between the two environments and begin to establish transactional constructivism with similar content in differing environments.[6] Transactional constructivism contends that knowledge is developed between the individual and the environment. The environment can include context, teacher, and peer influences. For example, an after-school program or competitive youth team may use a field space at a local school for soccer activities. However, the experience would be more meaningful if the activities were supported by a concurrent soccer unit within the physical education class. Communication between the after-school staff and the physical education department concerning unit plans, schedules, and learning objectives can enable the activities to be mutually beneficial. Students participating in both environments will have an enhanced educational experience with a congruent recreational experience. The outcomes could include higher performance on the National Standards for Physical Education, as well as advanced instruction and participation within the leisure experience.

An example of congruent programming has been noted in the development of goal-setting skills within afterschool programs.[7] Participants are provided opportunities to develop individual and group goals associated with three categories of their life: Home, School, and Community. School goals are established with academic subject areas so that the after-school program supplements specific activities during the regular school day. Individual goals focus on areas in which additional support is needed or warranted. In return, regular school day teachers provide evaluations to the afterschool program regarding progress toward those goals over an extended period of time.

Students begin to make the connections that school expectations are not divested activities compartmentalized within the school building. Rather, it is appropriate to pursue learning and growth opportunities in other venues and contexts as well.

A limitation of the congruent programming stage is that although an educational experience may be coordinated in terms of time, the delivery and objectives of the experience may vary. In the soccer example, a physical education teacher may encourage all students to learn each position and develop individualized skills

NEW DIRECTIONS FOR YOUTH DEVELOPMENT • DOI: 10.1002/yd

and affinity for the game. However, students participating on a competitive team after school may begin to be positioned so that their strengths contribute to the success of a team. The expectations for individual students might differ or even conflict. Transactional constructivism suggests that the meaning developed by individual students will differ for each participant. Nonetheless, the connection between formal academic experiences in school and leisure experiences beyond the school day cannot be overstated.

Infusion

A higher level of integration involves infusing each experience with the objectives of another. The purpose of infusion is to draw up the strengths of each activity with strong connections among each. Infusion requires extensive planning before units of instruction (or even academic years) begin. Many teachers are comfortable developing themes for academic years among grade levels or even within an entire school. However, extending a coordinated theme outside the school can strengthen these connections even further. For example, Mohnsen describes an integrated theme, "Taking Acceptable Risks."[8] Inherent within this theme is the encouragement of students to take appropriate chances and develop the self-confidence to do so. In addition, participating students can begin to differentiate between acceptable and unacceptable risks. School subjects that can explore this theme include military strategies in history, Food and Drug Administration processes in science, and the use of actuary tables for the development of math skills. However, infusing this theme into a community partnership with a local parks and recreation department, for example, may help deepen participation in low and high ropes activities or other forms of "risk recreation." Participating students can begin to see the connections from school-based activities with regard to acceptable risk taking while also acknowledging transferability within coordinated out-of-school experiences. The conceptualization of acceptable risk taking is seen as not only a school-based skill but also a life skill. In this way, youth can make connections to thematic elements and concepts rather than individualized skills and activities.

Among the limitations of infusion is the requirement for a high level of coordination and communication from the beginning of an educational or leisure experience to maximize its potential. Stakeholders and practitioners need to have buy-in to the process in order to achieve any level of fidelity for implementation. Leadership that includes a defined mission and vision is required for each entity to provide compatible experiences.

Integration

While the congruent programming and infusion stages work to coordinate in- and out-of-school activities and outcomes but still fundamentally work as different delivery systems, an effective integration stage views in- and out-of-school activities as linked learning and developmental opportunities for a child. Indeed, out-of-school-time programs can have a positive impact on the personal, academic, and social lives of youth participants.[9] Integrated out-of-school-time principles and activities should be embedded in the context of school reform efforts so that the potential impact of both can be realized. Successful integration is evidenced in the choices made outside of school and other formal programming as the child has integrated them into daily life. The choices for productive leisure pursuits are then linked to the in- and out-of school programming for which the teachers and staff members have been positioned as brokers.

Consider reading as an example. Reading is a requisite skill taught in school and measured by classroom and standardized tests. In an attempt to encourage reading beyond the school day, incentive programs such as Book It and the Accelerated Reader program have been deployed in many of our nation's schools.[10] As implemented, many students participate in reading incentive programs, and evidence suggests that reading achievement can be encouraged in this manner.[11] However, a disconnect occurs when a student chooses to read as a leisure activity but limits her selections to the Accelerated Reader book list, or when she stops reading after twenty minutes because that is the general expectation of the Book It program. The resulting outcome for participating in programs designed for inculcating a love for reading may actually obtain the opposite effect.[12] The education-for-leisure concept within the integration stage would remove the extrinsic barriers associated with reading, so that youth would choose to read because they are interested in the content and because they enjoy it.

Another example is participation in physical activity. Many states have physical activity standards that exceed those that can be achieved through physical education programs alone. For example, in South Carolina, state standards require elementary school students in grades K-5 to have 150 minutes of physical activity per week, 90 of which should come from physical education programs delivered by certified physical education teachers. The gap between that which should be achieved by the formal physical education program and the overall physical activity goals should be closed by "before, during, and after school dance instruction, fitness trail programs, intramural programs, bicycling programs, walking programs, recess, and activities designed to promote physical activity opportunities in the classroom."[13] All of these areas emphasize the role that free-choice leisure activities can play to meet state educational standards for physical activity and health.

At issue here is what is most important: the development of immediately assessable skills or the desire to choose regular participation in the activity. Certainly some level of skill is required for the development of intrinsically motivated participation. But the development of a skill itself may actually decrease the tendency for a youth to choose active participation during personal time. In the physical activity example, one of the national standards for physical education expects students to "achieve and maintain a health enhancing level of physical fitness."[14] Based on current time allocations for physical education in schools, additional activities outside a physical education class would be warranted to ascertain fitness. Indeed, another standard relates to "regular participation in physical activity." But if a student engages in physical activity to meet a school requirement, as in the submission of an exercise log, would he or she continue such participation after the semester was over?[15] And which would be more important: current fitness level or a sustaining motivational orientation toward physical activity?

Academic content is available for leisure pursuits among all subject areas. Sudoku, reading a science magazine, or engaging in the learning activities at a museum are a few examples. However, youth need assistance in bridging the gap between the learning and the leisure aspects of each. The integration stage makes this possible.

Self-determination theory

Self-determination theory (SDT) has been described as the degree to which an individual's behavior is self-motivated and self-determined.[16] In order to exhibit self-determination, one needs three components for that specific activity: autonomy, competence, and relatedness.[17] An effective teacher within a classroom has the ability to develop competence and relatedness within specific subject matter. For example, a math teacher can develop the mathematical skills of her students as well as meaningful interactions with and among her students in the classroom. However, any homework, project-oriented assignment, and even extra credit are by their very nature limited in their potential for autonomous engagement. Therein lies the need for the school to serve as the nexus of content development and the requirement for other resources to be engaged for accomplishment of self-determination.

In the previous physical education example, a class of students may participate in running as a warm-up or even a unit of activity. Free-choice participation in a local fun run or five-kilometer road race would be evidence of self-determined participation. A physical education teacher with an education-for-leisure orientation would seek opportunities for students to participate in a self-directive way and connect with community resources to provide those opportunities. Concurrently, community agencies such as recreation departments and after-school programs should establish similar connections with the local school. Similarly, a writing teacher might require extensive writing exercises as part of her class and provide feedback for assessment and skill development. However, the teacher might also make resources available to students that could enable them to showcase their skills in a writing competition or set up their own blog, which they might update on their own time. This would reveal tendencies toward self-determination. In each of these examples, the teacher must connect with resources outside the school environment.

Assessment instruments can be used to determine progress toward education for leisure such as the Motivation to Read Profile.[18] This instrument assesses recreational reading from a self-report inventory and a conversational interview. Finally, anecdotal data could be the most powerful indicators of all. Youth who volunteer information to a teacher or youth development professional about self-selected activities that align with intentional learning activities provide evidence that education for leisure is being accomplished.

Conclusion

Schools are places where students spend a large amount of time, and school environments influence multiple cognitive and noncognitive outcomes. School activities can contribute to adolescent resilience and positive development, and they have resources that can be put toward system change with regard to youth development.[19] Schools have the opportunity to focus on both academic and nonacademic outcomes, including promoting multiple areas of competence, character, connections to others, caring, and contribution to society. Such approaches can enhance the academic process. The potential for realizing these outcomes lies in the connection to student opportunities beyond the school day.

Constructing bridges to productive activities that complement expected outcomes in cognitive, physical, and social areas requires coordinated efforts among school personnel and community resources. Only then can we return to the original concept outlined by the Greeks and Dewey in which leisure pursuits constitute our greatest learning opportunities. Accepting an education-for-leisure mission can enable us to go back to the future with intentional learning activities.

Notes

1. Dewey, J. (1916). *Democracy and education.* New York, NY: Macmillan.
2. Department of the Interior. (1928). *Cardinal principles of secondary education: A report of the Commission on the Reorganization of Secondary Education, appointed by the National Education Association.* Washington, DC: Government Printing Office.
3. Darling-Hammond, L. (2010). *The flat world and education.* New York, NY: Teachers College Press.
4. Dustin, D. L., McKenney, A., Hibbler, D. K., & Blitzer, L. (2004). Thinking outside the box: Placing park and recreation professionals in K-12 schools. *JOPERD: The Journal of Physical Education, Recreation & Dance, 75*(1), 51–54.
5. Baker, T., & Masud, H. (2010). Liability risks for after-hours use of public school property to reduce obesity: A 50-state survey. *Journal of School Health, 80*(10), 508–513; Kennedy, M. (2006). Joining forces. *American School and University, 78*(9), 16–23.
6. Biesta, G.J.J., & Burbules, N. C. (2003). *Pragmatism and educational research.* Lanham, MD: Rowman & Littlefield.
7. Hallenbeck, A., & Fleming, D. (2011). Don't you want to do better? Implementing a goal-setting intervention in an afterschool program. *Afterschool Matters, 13*(1), 38–48.
8. Mohnsen, B. (2008). *Teaching middle school physical education: A standards-based approach for Grades 5–8* (3rd ed.). Champaign, IL: Human Kinetics.
9. Gomez, B. J., & Ang, P. (2007). Promoting positive youth development in schools. *Theory into Practice, 46*(2), 97–104.
10. Fawson, P. C., & Moore, S. A. (1999). Reading incentive programs: Beliefs and practices. *Reading Psychology, 20*(4), 325–340.
11. Konheim-Kalkstein, Y. L., & van den Broek, P. (2008). The effect of incentives on cognitive processing of text. *Discourse Processes: A Multidisciplinary Journal, 45*(2), 180–194.
12. Gambrell, L., & Marinak, B. (1997). Incentives and intrinsic motivation to read. In J. Guthrie & A. Wigfield (Eds.), *Reading engagement: Motivating readers through integrated instruction.* Newark, DE: International Reading Association; Kohn, A. (2010). How to create nonreaders: Reflections on motivation, learning, and sharing power. *English Journal, 100*(1), 16–22.
13. South Carolina. (2009). Physical education, school health services, and nutritional standards. South Carolina, sec. 59–10–10.

14. National Association for Sport and Physical Education. (2004). *National standards for physical education: Moving into the future* (2nd ed.) Reston, VA: Author.

15. Mitchell, M., Stanne, K., & Barton, G. V. (2000). Attitudes and behaviors of physical educators regarding homework. *Physical Educator, 57*(3), 136–145.

16. Deci, E., & Ryan, R. (2002). *Handbook of self-determination research.* Rochester, NY: University of Rochester Press.

17. Chirkov, V., Ryan, R. M., Kim, Y., & Kaplan, U. (2003). Differentiating autonomy from individualism and independence: A self-determination perspective on internalisation of cultural orientations, gender and well being. *Journal of Personality and Social Psychology, 84,* 97–110.

18. Gambrell, L. B., Palmer, B., Codling, R., & Mazzoni, S. (1996). Assessing motivation to read. *Reading Teacher, 49*(7), 518.

19. Gomez & Ang. (2007).

DAVID S. FLEMING *is an associate professor in the Eugene T. Moore School of Education at Clemson University.*

LAWRENCE R. ALLEN *is the dean of the College of Health, Education, and Human Development at Clemson University.*

ROBERT J. BARCELONA *is an assistant professor in the Youth Development Leadership Program at Clemson University.*

Community youth development is a transformative approach that can assist in a more equitable allocation of resources in programs that fail to engage low-income and minority urban youth.

4

Recreation as a component of the community youth development system

Corliss Outley, Jason N. Bocarro, Chris T. Boleman

IT TAKES A VILLAGE. The central assumption of this African proverb illustrates the role that communities can have in the development of young people. Youth today develop within nested systems that either positively or negatively influence their development. Recent research shows that American youth have made tremendous progress: fewer teen births, fewer youth who are heavy drinkers or smokers, and more students completing high school.[1] However, data also indicate that the number of youth living in poverty has increased steadily since 1998, an increasing number of children experience food insecurity, and the number of parents who are secure in their employment is the lowest since 1996.[2] These types of data have led many to wonder about the role the village, or community, has in providing support systems to youth.

Many educators and youth leaders seeking to solve the problems that youth face typically turn to the educational system. Unfortunately, schools have limited opportunities for youth voice and empowerment and often view these forms of healthy youth development as threats to institutional authority. The role of out-of-school-time programs is essential in the development of youth. Given that these programs are bound to communities and neighborhoods, we must begin to enlist community residents in efforts to create supportive and caring environments that have a common goal of positive youth development.

One area of the out-of-school-time sector is the provision of recreation services. Recreational services have a vital role in connecting youth to their communities as well as enabling youth and adult allies to improve challenging societal conditions. This article draws on years of theoretical and applied knowledge built on a set of specific assumptions:

- Youth operate in numerous and diverse contexts—at school, in the family, with peers, in their neighborhoods, as participants in youth programs, at faith-based institutions, in recreation, and even in the judicial system.
- Recreation centers and park areas, where many gangs and deviant youth congregate, are widely distributed across communities and can be used to deal with youth-related problems.
- Youth leaders are experienced in establishing supportive and caring relationships with their youth.
- Recreation activities are intrinsically appealing to large segments of youth and thus can attract diverse young people and have a positive influence on encouraging prosocial behavior.

To understand the role that recreation services have in community youth development, organizations and agencies must begin to help youth understand and participate in their communities and become agents of change.

NEW DIRECTIONS FOR YOUTH DEVELOPMENT • DOI: 10.1002/yd

Recreation in community youth development: A brief history

Leisure and recreation services have long been considered important to human and societal health. Our pastimes have played a pivotal role in civic engagement, assisted in the release from societal problems, and provided opportunities for family cohesion, social communication, and human and cultural development. The late 1970s and early 1980s saw trends that had a particular impact on youth development programs and how park and recreation departments have served youth. First, there was a sharp increase in the divorce rate in American families, which created more single-parent families and a subsequent increase in unsupervised and unstructured time for youth, particularly in communities where few free programs were offered. Second, budget cuts and constraints led to a deterioration of many recreation services.[3] Departments began to shift their emphasis away from addressing social concerns toward a more managerial profession, with expanding facilities and opportunities, guided by a philosophy of "recreation for all."[4] The oil embargos and taxpayer revolt of the late 1970s and early 1980s contributed to this shift, leading to recreation departments' becoming more business-like and entrepreneurial.

From the late 1980s to the early 1990s, events and conditions forced youth issues to the forefront of the political agenda: drive-by and school shootings, substantial increases in gang membership, increased teenage pregnancy rates, higher school dropout rates, growth in the number of low-income, single-parent households, and increased drug use.[5] Many public officials turned to park and recreation agencies for solutions due to the field's influence in the social reform movement and its historical access to youth within plagued communities.

Challenged by the needs in communities and encouraged by a renewed understanding of their own potential, park and recreation departments redefined their purpose. They have expanded their traditional (or perceived) boundaries as providers of "fun and games" to a more holistic youth-serving approach. To build on the strengths of its past and reinvent its public image, the recreation field has become more intentional about positioning itself in the youth development movement and the positive out-of-school-time debate. Current programmatic efforts include outdoor adventure, local sports lessons and leagues, arts and culture, gender and culturally specific opportunities, youth clubs, and direct contact through mentoring or peer groups.

Today the provision of recreation services in communities has extended beyond local municipalities to include an array of agencies and organizations. Major youth development providers include national organizations such as the Y, Boys and Girls Clubs, and 4-H; public agencies such as municipal park and recreation systems and libraries; sports organizations; private entities such as religious organizations and adult clubs; community institutions such as museums; and grassroots organizations that are home to individual youth groups or are attached to larger parent organizations.

Familiarity with leisure services gives youth and their families many choices about where to recreate, opportunities to engage in various forms of recreation, and increases in social interaction and community involvement. Yet studies have revealed that lower-income communities, both urban and rural, are the least likely to offer consistent support and a vast array of activities to their young residents.[6] Consequently many poor youth and their families cannot afford fee-for-service programs and rely on public and non-profit programs that offer free or low-cost activities. Unfortunately, these programs often lack sustained adequate funding.

Community-based youth development

The past decade has seen increasing interest in the meaningful involvement of youth in their communities. Referred to as community youth development (CYD), this approach has been defined as "purposefully creating environments that provide constructive, affirmative, and encouraging relationships that are sustained over time with adults and peers, while concurrently providing an array of opportunities that enable youth to build their own competencies and become engaged as partners in their own development as well as the development of communities."[7] In contrast to positive youth development, which focuses on the individual, the CYD approach requires long-term strategic planning and innovative plans of action that are collaboratively developed and implemented. Community youth development requires a holistic, strength-based approach that capitalizes on the potential contributions of youth-based programs to create and carry out an overall agenda for change in the community.

Community is often described as the settings, contexts, and social relations held within a geographical area among its people and its resources. Pittman states that the community—schools, community groups, religious organizations, places of employment, neighborhood resources, and the local job market—influences youth's developmental needs. She further states that affluent communities provide a richer diversity of activities and supports than what is available in communities with large numbers of families in poverty.[8] This inequality is frequently due to different social groups having access to disparate levels of social capital—access to networks that facilitate cooperation among and within groups— but also lead to social exclusion, heavy traffic, environmental degradation, and political powerlessness.

Community recreation-based programs can counter these negative neighborhood environmental conditions by contributing to the physical, social, emotional, and cognitive development of youth by providing a holistic strength-based approach that capitalizes on the potential assets that exist in each community. Communities need mobilization efforts to create conditions that encourage all stakeholders to engage in a strategic planning process on behalf of youth and their families.

Bringing the community together

The change in youth development practice over the past decades means that we must begin to critically envision what community youth development programs might look like. Camino and Zeldin set out three major themes that we believe provide the basic premise of what constitutes best practices for community youth development:[9]

- Identify and build on assets as well as needs
- Engage citizens and promote local control
- Create partnerships for capacity building and systemic change

These three themes center on the basic fundamental understanding of youth development and community development and focus on the values of citizen mobilization, youth empowerment, and shared power. The framework is a realignment of social, political, and economic capital that is designed to benefit all residents within a community.

Youth-serving organizations, regardless of type, must begin to work together to create the conditions necessary to provide supports and opportunities for youth and their families. Applying a positive youth development approach in communities is not an easy task. We provide an overview of each theme and present case study efforts that have achieved significant results.

Theme 1: Identify and build on assets as well as needs

The ability to identify the assets and the needs of young people is paramount. Youth development organizations should emphasize responding to the needs and issues that affect the local community. The primary focus is to build on the assets of individual youth as well as the resources within the community to assist in preparing youth to become productive adults. Communities must be able to identify and then access untapped resources—previous unacknowledged community leaders, financial sources, and spaces and places—in order to create and sustain a community's capacity, for example. The role of the community is to build future productive and well-functioning adults and must go beyond providing just programs and services.

Past efforts have frequently focused on community deficits and not the local realities. Better youth-based organizations focus on identifying and building on local assets. These assets are embedded in a community's residents, businesses, nonprofits, local government, and individual residents and are leveraged to address poverty, public health issues, human services, education, and criminal justice issues. By identifying assets and inviting organizations and individuals to contribute, we can begin to energize the community. For example, community youth mapping can be used to provide a detailed inventory of strengths, and the process aims to build trust and leads to immediate improvement efforts (see http://www.communityyouthmapping.org for an example).

Furthermore, the assets that exist within cultural and ethnic groups must also be acknowledged. Diversity in the United States consists of varying languages, cultures, ethnic groups, family types, abilities, and worldviews. The goal of community youth development within this realm is to help youth value cultural differences and assist in their own individual and cultural identity. Well-trained staff can create an atmosphere that acknowledges all youth and enable them to feel supported and empowered. By acknowledging and assisting in the development of identity, we can provide better supports and programmatic opportunities to youth from diverse backgrounds.

In Minneapolis, the Youthline Outreach Mentorship program was established in 1991 to involve local twelve- to sixteen-year-olds in positive leisure-time activities and encourage a sense of belonging in the community. The program consists of community involvement, creative expression, life skills for leadership development, outdoor adventure skill building, and cultural field trips. The program works by having local Youthline mentors at each park engage a core group of youth each week. The local mentors focus on getting to know the youth, establishing a positive relationship, and involving them in nearby activities that the local youth themselves determine. In addition, Youthline staff are directed to engage the local community to determine the resources available to youth.

A key to community youth development is identifying issues affecting the entire community. Minneapolis recently was hit by high levels of violence and negative behavior in the North Minneapolis neighborhood.[10] In response, two new programs were established: Youthline StreetReach teams and the Gang Prevention Intensive Mentoring Program.

Youthline has partnered with the City of Minneapolis Youth Diversion and Hennepin County's Juvenile Diversion program to have youth who are involved in the court or juvenile probation system referred to Youthline to complete their community service and, more important, connect them with adult mentors and positive recreational activities in order to keep them out of the juvenile justice system. The gang prevention program requires each Youthline mentor to connect with his or her mentee for at least two hours a week for three years. Currently more than fifty young people are involved in the program at thirteen parks, which has been funded by a federal grant for approximately $400,000 over three years.

The StreetReach teams provide mentorship, support, and resources to disengaged youth on the streets and at various gathering sites to encourage involvement in positive activities and assist in their developing better decision-making skills. The Youthline mentors concentrate on neighborhoods that were most involved in the recent violence.

This program illustrates how an organization responds not only to programmatic issues that affect youth residents but the entire community.

Theme 2: Engage citizens and promote local control

The aim of this theme is to create social capital within communities so that local stakeholders can take control of local issues. Critical to healthy youth development is the opportunity to build sociopolitical capacity, which emphasizes connections between common community problems and broader political and social issues. This assists in shaping youth's worldviews about the systemic causes of community problems and encourages them to work toward equity, fairness, and social justice. The community youth development approach assists youth in developing their skills as organizers and activists, which subsequently builds on a community's capacity to develop social capital. Ginwright states that community capacity occurs when youth work collectively with adults on community issues; develop alliances with institutions, organizations, and individuals; and ultimately shape policies to improve the community.[11]

The ability to work collectively with adults helps facilitate their development from dependence to interdependence. Youth civic participation requires adults to alter their view of the roles youth can undertake in society, from youth leaders advocating for them to youth being empowered to organize and lead on their behalf. This level of engagement in decision making and leadership increases skill development. In addition, youth who participate in community activities have reported more willingness to listen to others' points of view, value racial diversity, believe in the importance of helping those less fortunate, and view teamwork as important.[12]

By providing youth with opportunities to engage with the community, the Parker County 4-H program in Texas addressed a range of challenges and increased their sense of social responsibility and citizenship. In June 2009, Texas 4-H challenged all 254 counties in the state to make a difference in their communities by coming together on one day with service-learning projects of their choice to better their communities. Parker County 4-H Council was contacted by a representative of the Juvenile Diabetes Research Foundation about partnering in an effort to raise awareness and proceeds for type 1 diabetes research by hosting the 5K Walk to Cure Diabetes. The council was aware of at least three 4-H members who had been diagnosed with diabetes and decided this was the cause they needed to provide outreach to.

Parker County 4-H youth literally hit the ground running by organizing door-to-door and telephone campaigns to raise awareness for this event. 4-H ambassadors began researching type 1 diabetes and created an educational presentation to provide to local businesses, civic organizations, and county government to encourage their support and participation in the event. The Parker County 4-H Council and Ambassadors were the driving force behind this community project. Council members encouraged youth participation by providing presentations at youth-based organizational meetings and incorporating a competitive drive to see who could raise the most money. Efforts were also directed toward social media by encouraging friends to participate through Facebook, Twitter, and other social networks. The youth got community restaurants involved by offering spirit nights: 4-H members invited friends and family to eat out on designated evenings and the eating establishment donated a percentage to their cause. Youth also saw this as a recruitment opportunity for the 5K Walk to Cure Diabetes event by passing out educational flyers and inviting people to join the walk.

On the day of the event, the participating youth showed leadership by steering the event. They decorated the location, set up booths, and directed participants. As a result of their efforts, Parker County 4-H raised $105,000 for the Juvenile Diabetes Research Foundation and has continued to raise awareness of diabetes research throughout the community as an ongoing effort. (NOTE: Special thanks to Ms. Kayla B. Neill, County Extension Agent – 4-H and Youth Development, Parker County, Texas for providing this information.)

Theme 3: Create partnerships for capacity building and systemic change

Community building is generated through collaboration among diverse stakeholders across fields and sectors. The aim is to create long-term commitments that result in sustainable change in structures and systems, formal and informal. Community partnerships provide a way for organizations, individually and collectively, to influence policy, the community, and individual youth behavior. In addition, at the community level, organizations are able to more effectively coordinate and mobilize community resources, reducing competition and duplication of services.

During difficult economic times, youth-serving agencies often experience multiple challenges. Not only are financial resources diminished by reduced giving, but demand for programs and services often increases. Strategies that include public-private partnerships can result in a pooling of resources to address a mission relevant to their common constituency while meeting increasing demands for community youth services.[13] In 2009, a public-private partnership was created in Wake County, North Carolina, with the Boys & Girls Clubs (BGC), the Carolina Hurricanes Kids 'n Community Foundation, and the Capital City Crew (a local nonprofit organization). With funding from the National Hockey League Players Association's Goals and Dreams Foundation, North Carolina State University, and the Carolina Hurricanes, the Capital City Crew, a community youth development service organization, implemented an eight-week hockey instruction program to thirty-five children from a local BGC chapter. Participants were children aged eight to thirteen from low-income households in Wake County. Each participant was provided with a full set of hockey equipment and participated in eight one-hour on-ice sessions delivered by volunteer coaches from the Raleigh Youth Hockey Association working alongside high school and college student mentors who implemented a life skills component. The success of the program resulted in the program expanding to seventy participants the following year.

As youth sport opportunities become increasingly inaccessible, especially to children from disadvantaged families, children become more sedentary and fail to develop a repertoire of skills for recommended levels of leisure-time physical activity. Research has shown that youth from families living on low incomes participate in less physical activity and sport compared to youth from families with middle to high incomes.[14] As a result, numerous youth within the county have no opportunity to experience the benefits associated with sport participation.

This program not only offers a unique combination of sport skill instruction with life skill lessons to underserved youth, it also incorporates best practices for positive youth development programs. Too often initiatives such as sport instruction programs fail to achieve their full potential. Although the Capital City Crew program certainly has the capacity to develop sport skills in a previously underserved population in Wake County, its partnership with the Carolina Hurricanes gives it the ability to achieve much more. When sport introduction includes direct contact with professional athletes, especially at the local level, the learning environment is significantly stronger. Children are more attentive and more responsive, and typically they are willing to work harder. A hockey instruction program thus becomes a rich environment to implement and study the idea of using sport instruction as a platform to teach transferable life skills.

Where does this leave us?

Each of the best practice themes and case studies illustrates that the role of recreation in community youth development is changing. The focus has shifted from a fun-and-games mentality to a more deliberate strategy that places more value on the development of the community as a whole, in addition to individual well-being. Each of these programs drew on local capacities and resources that reflected concern for their community and the importance of community youth development to assist in developing a healthier environment.

The ideas of citizen engagement, empowerment, and shared power have become rallying cries across the nation. Community youth development is a fundamental change in how we provide services and opportunities for young people. It is based on all sectors working in an atmosphere of trust, cooperation, and respect.

We see these three best practice themes as paving the way toward greater acceptance of a community-centered approach to youth development in the area of out-of-school time.

Notes

1. Federal Interagency Forum on Child and Family Statistics. (2010). *America's children in brief: Key national indicators of well-being, 2010.* Washington, DC: U.S. Government Printing Office.

2. Federal Interagency Forum on Child and Family Statistics. (2010).

3. Bembry, R. (1998). A youth development strategy: Principles to practice in recreation for the 21st century. *Journal of Park and Recreation Administration, 16*(2), 15–34.

4. Sessoms, H. D. (1993). Justification for our services. *Trends, 30*(4), 6–8.

5. Witt, P. A., & Crompton, J. L. (1996). *Recreation programs that work for at-risk youth: The challenge of shaping the future.* State College, PA: Venture Publishing.

6. Quinn, J. (1999). Where need meets opportunity: Youth development programs for early teens. *Future of Children, 9*(2), 96–116.

7. Perkins, D.F., Borden, l., Keith, J., Hoope-Rooney, T., & Villarruel, F. (2003). Community youth development: Partnership creating a positive world. In F. Villarruel, D. Perkins, L. Borden, & J. Keith (Eds.), *Community youth development: programs, policies, and practices* (pp. 1–24). Thousand Oaks, CA: Sage Publications. P. 6.

8. Pittman, K. (1991). *Promoting youth development: Strengthening the role of youth serving and community organizations.* Washington, DC: Academy for Educational Development.

9. Camino, L., & Zeldin, S. (2002). From periphery to center: Pathways for youth civic engagement in the day-to-day life of communities. *Applied Developmental Science, 6*(4), 213–220.

10. Jenkins, E., Oliver, W., Poe, M., & Williams, O. (2009). *North Minneapolis Community Violence report.* Institute on Domestic Violence in the African American Community. Retrieved from http://www.idvaac.org/media/publications/NorthMinneapolicCommunityViolenceReport.pdf.

11. Ginwright, S. (2003). *Youth organizing: Expanding possibilities for youth development.* Brooklyn, NY: Funders' Collaborative on Youth Organizing. Retrieved from http://www.fcyo.org/media/docs/4243_Papers_no3_v3.qxd.pdf.

12. Hunter, S., & Brisbin, R. A. (2000). The impact of service learning on democratic and civic values. *Political Science* and *Politics, 33,* 623–626.

13. Yancey, A., Winfield, D., Larsen, J., Anderson, M., Jackson, P., Overton, J., ... Kumanyika, S. (2009). "Live, learn and play": Building strategic alliances between professional sports and public health. *Preventive Medicine, 49*(4), 322–325.

14. Lowry, R., Kann, L., Collins, J. L., & Kolbe, L. J. (1996). The effect of socioeconomic status on chronic disease risk behaviors among US adolescents. *Journal of the American Medical Association, 276*(10), 792–797.

CORLISS OUTLEY *is an associate professor of urban youth development in the Department of Recreation, Park, and Tourism Sciences at Texas A&M University.*

JASON N. BOCARRO *is an associate professor in the Department of Parks, Recreation, and Tourism Management at North Carolina State University.*

CHRIS T. BOLEMAN *is the program director for Texas 4H and Youth Development.*

Growth in the volume and rigor of camp research over the past decade has led to improved understanding of the value of the camp experience as a setting for positive youth development and the developmental outcomes of camp experiences for youth and adults, suggesting innovations and opportunities in the exploration of the camp experience.

5

Youth development and the camp experience

Barry A. Garst, Laurie P. Browne, M. Deborah Bialeschki

THE ORGANIZED CAMP experience has been an important part of the lives of children, youth, and adults for over 150 years and is a social institution that touches more lives than any other except for schools.[1] From the beginning, the camp experience has been a way for young people to explore and search for an authenticity often missing in other parts of their lives that contributes to their healthy transition into adulthood. Although camps vary in their mission, goals, and objectives, there is great similarity in basic camp values, such as connecting with nature, group living experiences, fun, meaningful engagement, personal growth, and skill development.

Camp is more than a location or a program; it encompasses the affective, cognitive, behavioral, physical, social, and spiritual

NEW DIRECTIONS FOR YOUTH DEVELOPMENT, NO. 130, SUMMER 2011 © WILEY PERIODICALS, INC.
Published online in Wiley Online Library (wileyonlinelibrary.com) • DOI: 10.1002/yd.398

benefits that youth receive during and after the camping experience. Over the past decade, tremendous growth in the volume and rigor of camp-related research has occurred, facilitated by a targeted research agenda conducted by the American Camp Association (ACA).[2] This agenda was founded on three national research projects conducted between 2003 and 2007: a study to identify the developmental outcomes of the camp experience, a benchmarking study of the youth development supports and opportunities provided through camp experiences, and a program improvement project directed toward enhancing supports and opportunities provided by camps.[3] Other national youth-serving agencies, such as 4-H, Boy Scouts of America, YMCA of the USA, and Girl Scouts of the USA, have also made important contributions to this body of knowledge. With these studies as a guide, this article explores the settings, structures, and program characteristics that appear to contribute to specific positive youth development experiences in camps, the developmental outcomes associated with camp experiences, and emergent innovations and opportunities in the study of camp experiences.

Supports and opportunities for positive youth development in camps

One way that a youth program provider might effectively target positive youth development (PYD) is by offering ample supports and opportunities for its participants. Supports include the people, programs, and intrapersonal skills that allow young people to seek new information and test their existing knowledge in a safe environment. They foster a young person's natural growth trajectory by providing elements essential to this process, such as supportive relationships with staff. A supportive program climate, for example, promotes social inclusiveness, thereby supporting youth's needs for belonging with a program setting. Opportunities foster positive development by offering novel, challenging, and engaging experiences that effectively open the learning pathways of young people. Opportunities offer pathways by which youth participants might test and apply new knowledge and skills, which facilitate outcomes such as skill building, competence, and a sense of mattering. Together these supports and opportunities encompass the variety of ways a youth development program might foster healthy growth among its participants.

Researchers have studied effective experiences built on supports and opportunities in a number of youth settings, and in general, programmatic supports and opportunities have a positive effect on youth development in these settings.[4] Using the Community Action Framework for Youth Development,[5] the ACA and Youth Development Strategies, Inc. (YDSI) examined the extent to which camp offers the supports and opportunities critical to healthy adolescent development.[6] During summer 2004, 7,645 boys and girls ages ten to eighteen who were attending one of eighty day or resident camps completed questionnaires to measure four domains of developmental supports and opportunities: supportive relationships, safety, youth involvement, and skill building. The results indicated that the greatest strength of camp was supportive relationships between youth and adult staff.[7]

Caring, supportive adults are critical to PYD since many children lack access to these types of adults because of fractured families, time constraints, and the erosion of neighborhood ties.[8] As indicated by ACA's Inspirations study, youth campers identified supportive relationships with camp staff as central to quality camp experiences. For example, in the Inspirations study, ACA found that 50 percent of camps had staff-to-camper ratios of one-to-three. Appropriate ratios allow ample opportunities for positive and meaningful interactions with adults. Furthermore, low staff-to-camper ratios may also play an important role in maintaining an emotionally and physically safe environment. The provision of safe places is foundational to all PYD settings, and most camps prioritize safety within their programs. One way the ACA supports these efforts is through its accreditation process.[9] Standards for camp operations and programming provide a framework from which camps might further support positive development among campers.

Camp characteristics that promote positive youth development

Research indicates that camps provide the supports and opportunities needed for PYD. Examining specific characteristics of the supports and opportunities afforded by camp experiences, including settings, structures, and programs and activities, provides a clearer understanding of camp as a PYD experience.

Setting characteristics

Camp experiences occur in settings characterized by unique features related to nature and time, which may play a particularly important role in shaping how camp experiences affect youth and adults.[10] A considerable body of research suggests that natural environments are contexts for personal restoration, referred to as a reduction in stress, arousal, and anxiety.[11] Restorative settings promote a sense of being away, that is, a change in the location and activities of daily life, and restoration associated with natural settings is greater than restoration received from nonnatural settings. The importance of being away—or escape—has been well documented in the literature on outdoor experiences.[12] Camp involvement provides youth with the opportunity to escape their home environments and experience the novel camp setting. For example, the 93 percent of resident camps and 63 percent of day camps that are located in a nature-based setting allow youth to make meaningful connections with nature.[13] Since many youth lack ongoing contact with nature, the remoteness of a nature-based camp experience provides them with a high degree of novelty.[14] Because camps are often located in remote outdoor areas, camp experiences often contrast with the everyday setting in which many campers live.

Camp experiences are also sustained for greater periods of time than many other youth experiences that may be short or spread out over time. Day campers participate for up to eight hours a day for several days, and youth participating in resident camps are involved twenty-four hours a day for up to several weeks. These sustained experiences, which differ from many other common childhood experiences, have a duration, intensity, and breadth that may be particularly influential to developmental outcomes.[15] Sustained experiences are important because they provide time for a camp to achieve its youth development goals. Immersive camp experiences also provide ample time for camp staff to reinforce positive attitudes and behaviors.[16]

Structural characteristics

Structural components of the experience, such as camp norms, group organization, and traditions and rituals, are typically integrated into camp experiences to contribute to PYD. Norms are a camp structure that include rules for behavior, ways of doing things, values and morals, and obligations for service; they are part of high-quality youth experiences intentionally leading to PYD outcomes.[17] Youth may adopt camp norms and rules through parent communications before camp, behavioral expectations posted around the camp property, and the ways that camp personnel demonstrate consistency and commitment to the camp policies. Camps establish norms through staff recruitment and training programs that teach staff how to model the camp's desired norms.[18] In addition, positive peer pressure supports adherence to camp norms, as do supportive relationships with camp staff. ACA's research into program improvement in camps reflects the importance of high, clear, and fair normative standards as a component of quality supports and opportunities.[19]

Group living is another important characteristic of camp experiences. At camp, children experience just about all aspects of their lives—eating, sleeping, playing, and working—in social groups. Successfully organizing children and adolescents in camp communities that can be as large as a small town is a key structural component of many camp experiences. Creating group cohesion using effective organization strategies is important because a natural tendency exists for individuals to favor certain individuals (over others) after they have been divided into groups. Many camp strategies, including similar group clothing, creative group names, group symbols, and group language (for example, slogans, songs, and chants), foster a sense of community in organizational settings.[20] These organizational elements have a positive influence on campers' self-identity.

Erikson's life cycle model of human development suggests that as young people move from childhood to adulthood, they consciously create a multidimensional image of their self, and they look to have their identity validated by others.[21] As youth leave their homes and neighborhoods to enter into a camp community, they have an opportunity to leave their personal baggage (poor choices, bad decisions, negative influences from friends at home) at the camp entrance. Camp is thus an equalizing context for youth. Many of the status symbols for youth (for example, wearing certain clothing, possessing the latest gadgets and gear) are less prevalent at camp. Because campers eat the same food, participate in the same activities, and sleep in the same large, shared spaces, differences between the haves and the have-nots are minimized.

Research with adolescents suggests that young people reinvent themselves through the camp experience by escaping the negative impressions of others and revising their self-identity at camp.[22] Undesirable personal characteristics can be shed in favor of new ways to think, feel, believe, and express themselves. Through camp groupings, campers also have opportunities to explore different social roles and build social capital.[23] Supportive relationships through group living with peers and the presence of caring adults, combined with setting characteristics such as sustained experiences, foster deep friendships with peers and adults and therefore a sense of belonging and connectedness.[24]

Traditions and rituals, such as opening ceremonies, competitive events, campfires, and even leadership programs, are some of the universal influential elements of the camp experience. Traditions and rituals foster group cohesion and community building, and they connect youth and staff to camps as special places. Because traditions recognize both the passage of time and change over time, they convey the impact of the past on the present and the future.[25] Positive experiences and memories, such as awards received or performances shared, become associated with camp traditions and rituals over time and are imbued with emotional significance. Traditions and rituals may also provide youth with additional opportunities for meaningful involvement, an important component PYD in camps. Campfire ceremonies are a common feature of the camp experience and an important example of traditions and rituals. Ceremonies like campfire programs foster personal reflection and recognition that appear to strengthen camp participants' connection to the camp community.[26] Campfires become symbolic and foundational to the construction of shared memories and storytelling.

Leadership development is another type of ritual in many camps, an important rite of passage that signals progression from childhood to adolescence to adulthood.[27] Leadership scaffolding, the creation of leadership development programs and opportunities such as counselor-in-training and leadership-in-training programs, is one example of how camps integrate rituals with program components.[28] Scaffolding provides intermediate leadership opportunities that serve as a mechanism for recognizing both the age and developmental differences of youth and their progression as they develop knowledge, skills, and abilities toward mastery.

Program and activity characteristics

In their review of prominent youth development programs, Roth and Brooks-Gunn found that the most effective programs offered primarily structured activities and limited the amount of unstructured time.[29] Unstructured time is one of the features that make camp distinctly different from other out-of-school-time programs, and recent studies suggest campers equate their most meaningful camp experiences to the time they spent outside structured activity. Hough and Browne found that campers gained skills and a sense of competence from camp activities, but developed a strong sense of social self-confidence and formed meaningful relationships during unstructured time.[30] It is possible that unstructured time, particularly when it is used intentionally to foster positive outcomes, is a unique way camps effectively promote positive youth development.

In contrast, structured camp activities promote youth development through features including experiential learning and choice. Direct, hands-on experience is a powerful medium for learning, and camp activities commonly provide youth with opportunities for holistic engagement.[31] By choosing activities in which to participate, campers are more likely to engage their intrinsic interests, a central component of youth development. It is not surprising that many campers report an overall sense of competence following their experience in camp activities.[32] Interestingly, they also highlight the opportunities for appropriate risk taking as a powerful means for personal growth at camp. Risk plays an important role in youth development, and many camps offer programs such as challenge courses and wilderness trips in order to safely support the learning and growth that occur as a result of positive risk taking. The experiential nature of camp activities, combined with the elements of choice, personal interest, skill development, and risk taking, allows structured camp activities to promote positive youth development.

Developmental outcomes of the camp experience

The most dramatic shift in camp research in the past decade has occurred in the areas of measuring developmental outcomes of camp experiences and developing reliable and valid measurement approaches for these outcomes. Several developmental models have guided the study of youth outcomes in camps, including the Search Institute's forty assets model, the targeting life skills model, the five Cs of positive youth development, and the Community Action Framework for Youth Development.[33]

Youth developmental outcomes

The developmental outcomes of the camp experience are well documented.[34] One of the first large-scale efforts was ACA's National Youth Development Outcomes study, in which five thousand youth, staff, and parents from a representative national sample of camps were asked about the ways in which campers benefited from the camp experience. Results from this study indicated that campers experienced growth in a wide variety of areas, including self-esteem, peer relationships, independence, adventure and exploration, leadership, environmental awareness, friendship skills, values and decisions, social comfort, and spirituality.[35] In addition to providing evidence of the value of the camp experience, these results also supported existing youth outcomes studies from other youth-serving organizations, thereby situating camp as an important context for positive youth development.[36]

Staff developmental outcomes

Staff outcomes, like camper outcomes, are an increasingly recognized value of the camp experience. Each year, close to a quarter-million older adolescents and emerging adults work as staff in ACA-accredited day and resident camps, and a large percentage of these staff members return to work in camps over multiple summers.[37] Trained as frontline leaders, staff members (most often between eighteen and twenty-five years old) provide youth with supervision and instruction in camp activities, and they bear much of the responsibility for making camp a setting for positive youth development. Since these emerging adults are themselves part of the youth development continuum, documenting staff outcomes also is important for research and practice. Research on camp staff outcomes suggests that camp experiences may contribute toward young adults' becoming fully functioning adults, characterized by the ability to find employment, form a lasting and gratifying partnership, and become a community contributor.[38]

Research into the developmental outcomes of camp experiences for staff has generally explored outcomes for either young adult paid staff or older adolescent teen staff.[39] The most common developmental outcomes for staff can be described as instrumental learning, which includes social and life skills development, and transformative learning, which describes how camp experiences promote deep change in young adult staff.[40] For example, camp staff report that they developed personal standards for their own behavior and learned to feel confident in showing their true personality and identity at camp.[41] Young adults who have worked at camp also appear to gain skills that affect their personal relationships, careers, and civic engagement outside camp. Two studies that focused on the long-term impacts of working at camp found that alumni staff believed that camp experiences contributed to twenty-first-century workforce skills such as planning, decision making, communication, and teamwork,[42] and that these experiences helped them explore new opportunities and try out new roles that they could apply in other settings.[43] Given the expansion of the definition of adolescence into the mid- to late twenties, many camp staff are in a developmental life stage much like the campers they serve.[44] Like camper outcomes, the duration and intensity of the camp experience may have a positive impact on young adults' transition into adulthood.

Measurement strategies for developmental outcomes in camps

The creation of PYD frameworks for understanding camp experiences has also led to the development of specific outcomes measurement approaches. Three such resources are the Tool Kit for Measuring Outcomes of Girl Scout Resident Camp, the National 4-H Camp Toolkit for Program Planning and Evaluation, and the ACA Youth Outcomes Battery.[45] ACA's Youth Outcomes Battery is a set of scales designed to be used by individual camps as a part of their evaluation efforts. The scales, developed and tested in day and resident camps, are age appropriate, reliable, and valid, and they allow camps to select which outcomes they want to target. To date, individual scales are available for friendship skills, responsibility, independence, family citizenship, teamwork, competence, exploration, affinity for nature, camp connectedness, problem-solving confidence, and spiritual well-being. Despite growth in the breadth of outcome measurement tools, survey research in camps can pose challenges. Short camp sessions, normal development (maturation), and demographics and individual differences can confound accurate measurement. Because of these limitations youth researchers have begun to investigate how a focus on quality program improvement might allow camp programs greater control over the processes that target developmental outcomes.[46] Program quality efforts acknowledge the role of outcomes while investigating aspects such as staff behaviors that are more under the control of the camp to influence through training and coaching.[47]

Conclusion

The expansion of our understanding of the camp experience over the past decade has been remarkable, and the emphasis on the developmental outcomes of camp experiences and the specific settings, structures, and programs and activities that foster positive youth development has been important and productive. The camp community has a much better appreciation for the fact that positive outcomes do not just occur because children attend camp; these desired outcomes must be planned, measured, and then incorporated into future program planning efforts. Although many more research questions must be answered in order to provide the field with practical strategies and resources to enhance program quality, the momentum built from this research has demonstrated the value and importance of the camp experience for positive youth development for all children.

Notes

1. Van Slyck, A. A. (2006). *A manufactured wilderness: Summer camps and the shaping of American Youth (1890–1960)*. Minneapolis, MN: University of Minnesota Press.

2. Bialeschki, M. D., & Conn, M. (2011). Welcome to our world: Bridging youth development research in non-profit and academic communities. *Journal of Research on Adolescence, 21*(1), 300–306.

3. American Camp Association. (2005). *Directions: Youth development outcomes of the camp experience.* Martinsville, IN: Author; American Camp Association. (2006a). *Inspirations: Developmental supports and opportunities of youths' experiences at camp.* Martinsville, IN: Author; American Camp Association (2006b). *Innovations: Improving youth experiences in summer programs.* Martinsville, IN: Author.

4. Catalano, R. F., Berglund, M. L., Ryan, J.A.M., Lonczack, H. S., & Hawkins, J. D. (2004). Positive youth development in the United States: Research findings on evaluations of positive youth development programs. *Annals of the American Academy of Political and Social Science, 591,* 98–124.

5. Gambone, M. A., Connell, J. P., Klem, A. M., Sipe, C. L., & Bridges, L. (2002). *Finding out what matters for youth: Testing key links in a community action framework for youth development.* Philadelphia, PA: Youth Development Strategies.

6. American Camp Association. (2006a).

7. Bialeschki, M. D., Henderson, K. A., & James, P. A. (2007). Camp experiences and developmental outcomes for youth. *Child and Adolescent Psychiatric Clinics of North America, 16,* 769–788.

8. Henderson, K. A., Bialeschki, M. D., Thurber, C., Schueler Whitaker, L., & Marsh, P. (2007). Components of camp experiences for positive youth development. *Journal of Youth Development, 3*(1), 17–28.

9. American Camp Association. (2007). *Accreditation standards for camp programs and services.* Martinsville, IN: Author.

10. Mannell, R. C., & Iso-Ahola, S. E. (1987). Psychological nature of leisure and tourism experience. *Annals of Tourism Research, 14,* 314–331.

11. Knopf, R. C. (1987). Human behavior, cognition, and affect in the natural environment. In D. Stokols & I. Altman (Eds.), *Handbook of environmental psychology.* Hoboken, NJ: Wiley; Hartig, T., Mang, M., & Evans, G. W. (1991). Restorative effects of natural environment experience. *Environment and Behavior, 23,* 3–26.

12. Kaplan, R., & Kaplan, S. (1989). *The Experience of nature: A psychological perspective.* Cambridge: Cambridge University Press.

13. American Camp Association. (2008a). *Camp sites, facilities, and programs report: 2008.* Martinsville, IN: Author.

14. Louv, R. (2005). *Last child in the woods: Saving our children from nature-deficit disorder.* Chapel Hill, NC: Algonquin Books.

15. Ferrari, T. M., & McNeely, N. N. (2007). Positive youth development: What's camp counseling got to do with it? Findings from a study of Ohio 4-H camp counselors. *Journal of Extension, 45*(2). Retrieved from http://www.joe.org/joe/2007april/rb7.php.

16. Garst, B., Franz, N., Baughman, S., Smith, C., & Peters, B. (2009). Growing without limitations: Transformation among young adult camp staff.

Journal of Youth Development, 4(1), 23–37; Powell, G., & Scanlin, M. (2002, September/October). Ways to promote youth development in camp. *Camping Magazine,* 14–17.

17. Smith, C., Devaney, T. J., Akiva, T., & Sugar, S. A. (2009). Quality and accountability in the out-of-school-time sector. In N. Yohalem, R. C. Granger, & K. J. Pittman (Eds.), *New Directions for Youth Development, 121.* Defining and measuring quality in youth programs and classrooms (pp. 109–127). San Francisco: Jossey-Bass; Roth, J., & Brooks-Gunn, J. (2000). What do adolescents need for healthy development? Implications for youth policy. *Social Policy Report, 14*(1), 3–19.

18. American Camp Association. (2006b).

19. American Camp Association. (2008a).

20. Rosenbaum, M. E., & Holtz, R. (1985). *The minimal intergroup discrimination effect: Outgroup derogation, not ingroup favoritism.* Paper presented at the 93rd Annual Convention of the American Psychological Association, Los Angeles; Bryk, A. S., & Driscoll, M. E. (1988). *The school as community: Theoretical foundations, contextual influences, and consequences for students and teachers.* Madison: University of Wisconsin.

21. Erikson, E. H. (1963). *Childhood and society* (rev. ed.). New York, NY: Norton.

22. Garst et al. (2009).

23. Yuen, F. C., Pedlar, A., & Mannell, R. C. (2005). Building community and social capital through children's leisure in the context of an international camp. *Journal of Leisure Research, 37,* 494–518; Cranton, P. (1994). *Understanding and promoting transformative learning: A guide for educators of adults.* San Francisco, CA: Jossey-Bass.

24. Gillard, A., Watt, C. E., & Witt, P. A. (2009). Camp supports for motivation and interest: A mixed-methods study. *Journal of Park and Recreation Administration, 27*(2), 74–96.

25. Jacobi, M., & Stokols, D. (1983). The role of tradition in group-environment relations. In N. R. Feimer & E. S. Geller (Eds.), *Environmental psychology: Directions and perspectives.* Westport, CT: Praeger.

26. Garst et al. (2009).

27. Bell, B. (2003). The rites of passage in outdoor education: Critical concerns for effective programming. *Journal of Experiential Education, 26,* 41–50; Dahl, T. I. (2009). The importance of place for learning about peace: Residential summer camps as transformative thinking places. *Journal of Peace Education, 6,* 225–245.

28. Larson, R., Hansen, D. M., & Walker, K. (2005). Everybody's gotta give: Adolescents' development of initiative within a youth program. In J. Mahoney, J. Eccles, & R. Larson (Eds.), *After-school activities: Organized activities as contexts of development* (pp. 159–183). Hillsdale, NJ: Erlbaum.

29. Roth & Brooks-Gunn. (2000).

30. Hough, M., & Browne, L. P. (2009). *Connecting camp mechanisms to camper outcomes: A case for program theory.* Paper presented at the National Conference of the American Camp Association. Orlando, FL.

31. Bialeschki et al. (2007).

NEW DIRECTIONS FOR YOUTH DEVELOPMENT • DOI: 10.1002/yd

32. American Camp Association. (2005); Hough & Browne. (2009); Roark, M. F. (2009). *Does the power of the camp experience differ within the length of sessions? An analysis of session length on camper developmental outcomes of competence, friendship skills, and independence.* Paper presented at the American Camp Association National Conference, Orlando, FL.

33. Benson, P. L. (2003). Developmental assets and asset-building communities: Conceptual and empirical foundations. In R. M. Lerner & P. L. Benson (Eds.), *Developmental assets and asset-building communities: Implications for research, policy, and practice* (pp. 19–43). New York, NY: Kluwer Academic/Plenum; Hendricks, P. A. (1998). *Targeting life skills model.* Ames: Iowa State University Extension; Lerner, R. M., Lerner, J. V., Almerigi, J. B., Theokas, C., Phelps, E., Gestsdottir, S., . . . & von Eye, A. (2005). Positive youth development, participation in community youth development programs, and community contributions of fifth-grade adolescents: Findings from the first wave of the 4-H study of positive youth development. *Journal of Early Adolescence, 25,* 17–71; Gambone et al. (2002).

34. Bialeschki et al. (2007); Thurber et al. (2007).

35. American Camp Association. (2005).

36. Garst, B., & Bruce, F. (2003). Identifying 4-H camping outcomes using a standardized evaluation process across multiple 4-H educational centers. *Journal of Extension, 41*(3). Retrieved from http://www.joe.org/joe/2003june/rb2.php; Boy Scouts of America. (2001). *Boy Scouts of America summer camp outcomes study.* Retrieved from http:www.scouting.org/FILESTORE/marketing/pdf/02-448-1.pdf; Arnold, M., Bourdeau, V. D., & Nagele, J. (2005). Fun and friendship in the natural world: The impact of Oregon 4-H residential camping programs on girl and boy campers. *Journal of Extension, 46*(6). Retrieved from http://www.joe.org/joe/2005december/rb1p.shtml.

37. American Camp Association. (2008a).

38. Furstenberg, F. E. (1999). *Managing to make it: Urban families and adolescent success.* Chicago: University of Chicago Press.

39. Colyn, L., DeGraaf, D., & Certan, D. (2008). Social capital and organized camping: It's about community. Camping Magazine, 81(2). Retrieved from http://www.ACAcamps.org/members/knowledge/participant/cm/0803socialcapital.php; DeGraaf, D., & Glover, J. (2002). Long term impacts of working at an organized camp for seasonal staff. Unpublished manuscript; James, J. J. (2003). The threshold for staff transformation: An ethnography of Girl Scout camp staff. Retrieved from http://acacamps.org/research/03symposium.pdf; Powell, G. M., Bixler, R. D., & Switzer, D. M. (2003). Perceptions of learning among new and returning seasonal camp staff. Journal of Park and Recreation Administration, 21(1), 61–74; Forsythe, K., Matysik, R., & Nelson, K. (2004). Impact of the 4-H camp counseling experience. Madison: University of Wisconsin-Extension, Department of Youth Development; Garst, B., & Johnson, J. (2005). Adolescent leadership skill development through residential 4-H camp counseling. *Journal of Extension 43*(5). Retrieved from http://www.joe.org/joe/2005october/rb5.php; Klem, M. D., & Nicholson, D. J. (2008). Proven effectiveness of Missouri 4-H camps in developing life skills in youth. *Journal of Youth Development, 2*(3), 132–139.

40. Lyons, K. D. (2000). Personal investment as a predictor of camp counselor job performance. *Journal of Park and Recreation Administration, 18*(2), 21–36; DeGraaf. (2008); Colyn et al. (2008); James. (2003); Powell et al. (2003); Forsythe et al. (2004; Garst & Johnson. (2005); Klem & Nicholson. (2008); Cranton. (1994); Garst et al. (2009).

41. Powell & Scanlin. (2002); Garst & Johnson. (2005).

42. Digby, J. K., & Ferrari, T. M. (2007). Camp counseling and the development and transfer of workforce skills: The perspective of Ohio 4-H camp counselor alumni. *Journal of Youth Development, 2*(2), 101–119.

43. Brandt, J., & Arnold, M. E. (2006). Looking back, the impact of the 4-H camp counselor experience on youth development: A survey of counselor alumni. *Journal of Extension, 44*(6). Retrieved from http://www.joe.org/ joe/2006december/rb1.php; Johnson, S.K., Goldman, J, A., Garey, A.I., Brtiner, P.A., & Weaver, S.E. (2011). Emerging adults' identity exploration: Illustrations from inside the "camp bubble." *Journal of Adolescent Research, 26*(2), 258–295.

44. Arnett, J. (2004). *Emerging adulthood: The winding road from the late teens through the twenties.* New York, NY: Oxford University Press; Bynner, J. (2005). Rethinking the youth phase of the life-course: The case for emerging adulthood. *Journal of Youth Studies, 8*(4), 367–384.

45. Girl Scouts of the USA. (2001). *Tool kit for measuring outcomes of Girl Scout resident camp.* New York, NY: Author; Garst, B., Nichols, A., Martz, J., McNeely, N., Bovitz, L., Frebertshauser, D., Garton, M., . . . Walahoski, J. (in press). Examining youth outcomes across multiple states: The National 4-H Camping Research Consortium. *Journal of Youth Development;* Ellis, G., & Sibthorp, J. (2006). *Development and validation of battery of age-appropriate measures for camper outcomes.* Martinsville, IN: American Camp Association.

46. American Camp Association. (2006b).

47. Walker, J., Gran, C., & Moore, D. (2009). *Once we know it, we can grow it.* Retrieved from http://www.extension.umn.edu/youth/docs/once-we-know-it-whitepaper.pdf.

BARRY A. GARST *is the director of program development and research application for the American Camp Association and adjunct professor at Virginia Tech.*

LAURIE P. BROWNE *is a graduate research assistant at the University of Utah in Salt Lake City.*

M. DEBORAH BIALESCHKI *is the director of research for the American Camp Association and professor emeritus from the University of North Carolina–Chapel Hill.*

For youth today to achieve their full potential, outdoor-based play and reconnection to nature are essential.

6

Outdoor-based play and reconnection to nature: A neglected pathway to positive youth development

Fran P. Mainella, Joel R. Agate, Brianna S. Clark

A RECENT PUBLICATION FROM a renowned child development specialist described a history of play that dates back to ancient times.[1] Archaeological digs have identified elements of play in ancient China, Peru, and Egypt, and anthropological studies have found evidence of playful activity even among primitive cultures.[2] Frost states that history's most prominent philosophers (including Plato), educators, and thinkers have viewed play as essential "to the development of a full childhood and a happy, well-developed person."[3] In spite of the historic and largely uninterrupted recognition of the importance of play in the development and success of children, history also tells of periods when play has been largely neglected or rejected by society.[4]

In the late nineteenth century, American children lacked opportunities to play due to crowded urban conditions and a reliance on child labor. In addition to the need for child labor, Curtis indicated

We thank Austin Barrett for his significant effort in researching and preparing the manuscript for this article.

that the increased demands of education and the overdevelopment of urban places left "little room for play" and that "play ha[d] probably reached the lowest ebb during the last half century that it ha[d] ever reached during the history of the world."[5] It was during these years that people in the United States started to take steps to provide access to play spaces.

The city of Boston opened an organized playground in one of its schoolyards as early as 1868. In 1886, the Boston Women's Club and the Massachusetts Emergency and Hygiene Association sponsored the first supervised playground in the United States, beginning the playground movement. As playgrounds and parks across the United States became more prevalent, a group of playground advocates, including Luther Gulick, Henry Curtis, and Joseph Lee, organized the Playground Association of America in 1906, which later became the National Recreation Association. This group and other associations called for the development of playgrounds and programs to provide children with opportunities for play.[6]

Play deprivation today

The increase of playgrounds in multiple settings provides evidence that the early playground movement has been successful. Unfortunately, modern American society faces challenges that are much different from those that the early pioneers of American play face. Play deprivation, or lack of play, is not a result of deficient play space; rather, for most children, it is their unwillingness to choose free and spontaneous outdoor play such as that which occurs in parks and other natural settings.

Play in parks and natural areas provides youth with the opportunity to encounter challenge and develop skills encountered in everyday life.[7] However, a lack of play in natural settings leads to not only play deprivation but also what Louv terms "nature deficit disorder."[8] Nature deficit disorder is a disconnection with the environment that stems from the current generation's tendency to focus on built and engineered entertainment rather than the natural world. Because of this disconnect, children miss nature's restorative effects, resulting in youth with weaker minds, bodies, and senses. Louv's critical examination of the state of children's nature-based play has sparked broad public interest in the human-nature connection and the role of outdoor play in the positive development of America's youth.

Children's play deprivation and lack of association with nature stem from many factors. One important factor is the rise of modern technology and increased media exposure. The proliferation of electronic media in American homes has provided alternative forms of recreation that are accessible with very little effort, and youth are flocking to these recreation resources. A recent study reports that youth between the ages of eight and eighteen spend an average of seven hours thirty-eight minutes each day with electronic media, totaling almost fifty-three hours each week.[9] No doubt the media have long been and will continue to be a permanent and evolving part of American life. Part of the challenge that youth development agencies face now and in the future is to find a balance between the influences of media (for example, gaming, television, Internet-based communications, and social networking) and the face-to-face human interactions that play provides.

A lack of outdoor play has been attributed as well to stranger danger, or the fear a parent may have of what might happen if a child is allowed to play outside.[10] A recent study of 830 mothers found that although 70 percent of today's mothers played outside daily when they were children, only 31 percent of them allow their children to do so today.[11] These parents indicated that concerns about crime and safety were a primary reason that they did not allow their children to play outside. In an era in which child abductions are sensationalized by twenty-four-hour media coverage and Amber Alerts, people have become conditioned to focus on the possibility of harm. Although the number of child abductions occurring today appears alarmingly high, research shows that the actual prevalence of such abductions and crimes against children has not grown in recent years.[12] The increased amount of media coverage over the past years has created an optical illusion, inflating the dangers associated with outdoor play. Similarly, Sutton states, "Stranger-danger is largely a myth promoted by the mass media, yet there are few voices raised against it."[13]

Another important contributor to play deprivation is what has been coined the hurried child or the overscheduled child.[14] Children today are often carted from soccer practice, to dance class, to piano lessons, and many other activities during their free time. Although structured activities have been shown to provide the greatest context for positive youth development, the structured activities that children engage in often take the place of the unstructured, outdoor-based, free play that children need.[15] In addition, freely chosen leisure experiences such as play have been shown to provide a significant role in youth development. Research has found that adolescents typically define their leisure by activities that are unstructured and highly social.[16]

Consequences of play deprivation

It is worth considering the consequences of a lack of play in the outdoors. Frost describes such consequences as "a growing crisis that threatens children's health, fitness, and development." He states on the US Play Coalition website (http://usplaycoalition. clemson.edu/), "As free outdoor play declines, fitness levels decline, waistlines expand, and a host of health problems follow, including obesity, heart disease, rickets, and a spiraling upturn in emotional and social disorders." Frost's understanding of these consequences is outlined in his recent work, which reviews the literature and outlines the cognitive, social, and physiological consequences of play deprivation today.[17] Brown and Vaughn argue similarly that the lack of play in people's lives has led to a decreased capacity to deal with the stressors of everyday life and rampant increases in emotional and psychological disorders.[18] Isolation from nature also results in increased obesity and associated health problems, diminished capacity to function socially, and increased stress levels that create negative outcomes in the lives of children, adults, and families.[19]

Evidence of lack of outdoor-based play

The research clearly indicates that youth today lack outdoor-based play. Numerous studies describe the disappearance of recess, unstructured outdoor-based play during the school day, in American schools.[20] Recent research on recess reveals that as many as 40 percent of U.S. school districts have either eliminated or significantly reduced recess time so as to make more time available for curriculum and instruction. A full quarter of American elementary schools offer no recess to some grade levels. A Gallup poll of approximately two thousand American principals and school administrators found that "principals overwhelmingly believe recess has a positive impact not only on the development of student's social skills, but also on achievement and learning in the classroom."[21] Nonetheless, 20 percent of these principals reported that high-stakes testing has caused them to cut back on recess time.[22] In addition, in the years since implementation of the No Child Left Behind Act of 2001, American schools have seen a 28 percent decrease in recess and a 35 percent decrease in physical education.[23]

This erosion of recess time and physical education is occurring in the face of widespread deficits in the physical activity of the American population. Research shows that one in four Americans engage in no physical activity during their leisure time.[24] A recent review of the research literature on children's physical activity and outdoor play reported that children today spend less time playing outdoors and do so with a smaller and less diverse group of playmates in a more restricted area. Not surprisingly, these children are spending more time indoors engaging with electronic media, and when they do go outside, adults often manage a structured activity for them. For reasons ranging from concerns about stranger danger, to a new infrastructure in which larger schools are built in decentralized locations, these children are also less likely to walk or bike to school.[25]

Why focus on outdoor-based play?

Many beneficial outcomes of play are documented in the research literature, and such benefits clearly span different aspects of development. Some of the benefits derived from play behaviors are easily recognized, like physical fitness and health-related outcomes, while others are less readily apparent. Some of the psychological, social, and educational benefits may even be considered counterintuitive. One example may be illustrated by the findings of a recent study. Barros, Silver, and Stein found that preteen students who have recess perform better in the classroom than do students who spend what would otherwise be used as recess time in traditional learning activities.[26] Regardless, play has been shown to greatly benefit the physical, mental, cognitive, and socioemotional health and development of youth.

Physical fitness and obesity

Our nation (and the world beyond) is facing an epidemic of childhood obesity and inactivity that is leading to a vast array of additional health concerns, including type 2 diabetes, cardiovascular disease, and adulthood obesity.[27] Current reports of childhood obesity rates for North American children fall between 20 and 35 percent.[28] This epidemic has left officials and health professionals looking for innovative strategies to address children's physical activity. Research abounds in support of the role of play in encouraging physical activity. For example, Pellegrini and Smith indicate that the lack of adult demands on children's play allows them to choose the types of physical activity that appeal to them.[29]

Mental health

Psychological and emotional health benefits also seem to be derived from outdoor free play. Recent studies have found a link between the lack of free play and the prevalence of emotional disorders, including anxiety and depression.[30] In a longitudinal study that consisted of 129 toddlers with delayed growth at nine to twenty-four months, the children were given either supplementation to enhance their growth or regular play sessions over a specified period of treatment. A sixteen-year follow-up of these children showed that those who engaged in play measured significantly higher in self-esteem and displayed significantly lower levels of anxiety, depression, and attention issues than those in the other treatment group.[31] Not only does play have the ability to reduce depression and anxiety, Kuo and Taylor found a significant link between outdoor play and the severity of symptoms in children with a diagnosis of attention deficit hyperactivity disorder (ADHD). Specifically, they found that the more exposure a child has to natural environments, the more manageable the symptoms of ADHD are.[32]

Cognitive development

While many view play as frivolous or even wasteful time that takes away from those things that are useful and productive, play indeed seems to make a significant contribution to cognitive and intellectual development. Scholars including Piaget and Vygotsky have linked play to cognitive development.[33] According to the American Academy of Pediatrics, play is essential to cognitive development. It gives children opportunities to explore their creativity, develop their imaginations and dexterity, and increase their physical, cognitive, and emotional strength.[34] Numerous researchers identify play as an essential part of healthy brain development.[35] Children use play to learn to engage with the world around them and thereby gain understanding, develop new competencies, and increase in confidence and capacity. According to Ginsburg, "It is becoming increasingly clear through research on the brain as well as in other areas of study, that childhood needs play. Play acts as a forward feed mechanism into courageous, creative, rigorous thinking in adulthood."[36]

Scholars indicate that among all the ways children learn, play may indeed be the most developmentally appropriate approach to learning.[37] Findings indicate that play contributes to advances in "verbalization, vocabulary, language comprehension, attention span, imagination, concentration, impulse control, curiosity, problem solving strategies, cooperation, empathy, and group participation."[38] Barros et al. found that children who are given recess, allowing them to play actively during the school day, display higher levels of classroom behavior (as rated by their teachers) and are better able to learn in a classroom setting.[39]

Socioemotional outcomes

A vast array of research describes the socioemotional benefits children derive from play. Scholars have suggested that play facilitates emotional and social skills.[40] Through play, children are able to cooperate and participate in social activities, and they practice emotional regulation, empathy, and group management skills.[41] They also have opportunities to practice sensing the perspectives of others and develop an understanding of emotions and emotional regulation.[42] Play has also been associated with children's understanding of the emotions others feel.[43] Children at play practice sharing, turn taking, self-restraint, group work, and simply getting along.[44]

A return to free and spontaneous outdoor play

The national attention that Louv has brought to the issue of nature deficit disorder and that others have brought to the forefront is notable. The distinct fading away of play has resulted in numerous programs and projects aimed at reversing the trend. Many have identified the lack of free and spontaneous outdoor play as a problem. Howard Frumkin, a former director of the National Center for Environmental Health in the U.S. Centers for Disease Control, said, "Evidence suggests that children and adults benefit so much from contact with nature that land conservation can now be viewed as a public health strategy."[45]

A number of programs now in place seek to implement this public health strategy through education and engagement. The remainder of this chapter outlines some of the programs and initiatives engaged in this effort.

Jr. Ranger Programs

The U.S. National Park Service (NPS), as well as many state park systems throughout the country, have implemented Jr. Ranger programs (http://www.nps.gov/learn/juniorranger.htm). These programs are designed to engage children as young as six years old in outdoor activities and environmental education. Youth are encouraged to explore, learn, and protect the parklands they visit. Many NPS units, including Acadia and Zion National Parks and Gettysburg National Military Park, also offer children's programming with hands-on activities to introduce children to the outdoor world.

Let's Move Outside

In 2010, First Lady Michelle Obama introduced Let's Move: America's Move to Raise a Healthier Generation of Kids (http://www.letsmove.gov; http://www.letsmove.gov/letsmoveoutside.php). The Let's Move campaign seeks to eradicate childhood obesity within a generation through food and nutrition education as well as efforts to increase the physical activity of all Americans. Included in this campaign are many references to the importance and value of play and a specific call for at least sixty minutes of active and vigorous play each day. A recently added branch of the Let's Move campaign is Let's Move Outside. The campaign advocates that playing outside is one of the easiest and most enjoyable ways to meet the goal of sixty minutes of activity. Let's Move Outside is a coordinated effort between the U.S. Department of the Interior and the U.S. Department of Agriculture "to get kids moving outside."

America's Great Outdoors

Another governmental effort that is underway is the America's Great Outdoors Initiative (http://www.doi.gov/americasgreatoutdoors), which seeks to involve the American public in sharing ideas to protect outdoor spaces. In addition, the program engages young people from various backgrounds by employing and educating them about public lands.

Natural Playground and Play Space Design

The Natural Learning Initiative (NLI) is making significant efforts to integrate natural elements into built environments and is conducting action research to reengage children with nature (http://www.naturalearning.org). This initiative identifies numerous causes for children's loss of contact with the natural world, including child care centers with outdoor spaces that do not support children's developmental needs. The organization argues that due to overly concerned parents, domestic air-conditioning, state-mandated testing, and overly scheduled children, children are prevented from spending time in the outdoors. In response to this lost connection, the NLI assists communities in recognizing the importance of natural play spaces creating such spaces.

Children and Nature Network

Another initiative that is advocating the return of free and unstructured outdoor play is the Children & Nature Network (C&NN; http://www.childrenandnature.org). Its focus is to encourage parents to take their children outdoors and provide opportunities for play.

C&NN has created a series of networks and tool kits aimed at developing a connection between children and nature. The Natural Families Network provides tool kits and resources that include how-to guides designed to help parents and community leaders assist in the creation of grassroots efforts to get people outside. In some cases, these grassroots efforts take the form of Nature Clubs for Families in which families in a local area come together to engage with nature. To date, C&NN has assisted over sixty communities in either launching or assembling grassroots campaigns to connect children with nature.

With the support of the Sierra Club, the C&NN makes available the Natural Leaders Network program, which provides tool kits that empower and encourage young people to become advocates for nature. The network also invites young people to bring their friends along. This program not only reconnects children, youth, and families with nature but also provides meaningful and developmental leadership experiences. The Natural Teachers Network provides a venue for teachers to share ideas, successes, and challenges that they face as they work to expose children to natural spaces. C&NN has also designated April as Children and Nature Awareness Month. In 2010 this event resulted in at least 506 events that were scheduled across the country to reconnect children and families with nature.

The US Play Coalition

In June 2009 a group of people came together in Clemson, South Carolina, for the Summit on the Value of Play. This group gathered under the belief that play is a basic human right on which strong intellectual, physical, and emotional development is built. Summit attendees addressed the physical, cognitive, and affective benefits of play and discussed the political and social barriers that impede access to play. At the end of the summit, attendees agreed on five calls to action that they would pursue in an effort to make play available to all:

1. To create a coalition for play to communicate and advocate for a new play movement. The US Play Coalition (http://usplaycoalition.clemson.edu), developed in response to this call, is a partnership to promote the value of play throughout life. The coalition consists of organizations and individuals with a diversity of backgrounds: educators, health professionals, parks and recreation professionals, psychologists, landscape architects, and many more. The coalition serves as a gathering

place for like-minded organizations that value play. The coalition is also charged with holding conferences on the value of play to better educate and network play advocates throughout the world.

2. To synthesize existing research on play as it affects a person's lifelong cognitive, physical, and affective development. Also of interest is research that identifies the costs to society and individuals that result from lack of play. Some of this research has been presented in this article, and more is available through the US Play Coalition.

3. To develop a robust national communications campaign promoting the play movement. Through this campaign, the coalition seeks to inspire families and individuals to change their perceptions and behaviors regarding the essential value of play.

4. To advocate for legislation in support of play. The US Play Coalition was among the first to speak out in support of the Let's Move campaign and the America's Great Outdoors initiative, and it continues to seek opportunities to be involved in shaping policy in support of play.

5. To develop national guidelines for healthy play and healthy communities, thereby making access to play-friendly communities easier across the nation.

The US Play Coalition continues to provide a partnership to promote the value of play throughout life through these efforts and more yet to come.

A neglected pathway to positive youth development

Outdoor-based play and reconnection to nature are critical if we wish to achieve positive youth development. The organizations we have described, along with others who have identified the developmental importance of the connection between youth and nature, are leading the fight against play deprivation and nature deficit disorder. It is also worth noting that these organizations and programs focus on the needs of not just youth because play deprivation is occurring during all life stages. While youth development generally addresses the needs of adolescents, the developmental and beneficial nature of play is most often experienced during childhood. Evidence abounds that people today, regardless of age, are losing the important connection to nature that has existed and contributed to positive development throughout history. Evidence also abounds that people are experiencing a level of play deprivation that is not unlike that children experienced in the late nineteenth century. At that time, a few caring citizens joined together to address the problem, and the first play movement was born. Today we are at an equally important decision point. Frost indicated that the crisis of play deprivation calls for a "massive coordinated effort"(http://usplaycoalition.clemson.edu/). The groups we have noted are engaging in that effort, but more coordination is needed, and those concerned with youth development are in a unique position to intervene in a powerful way.

Notes

1. Frost, J. (2009). *A history of children's play and play environments: Toward a contemporary child-saving movement*. New York, NY: Routledge.
2. Mitchell, E. (1937). *The theory of play*. Baltimore, MD: Penguin Books.
3. Frost. (2009). P. 9.
4. Curtis, H. (1917). *The play movement and its significance*. New York, NY: Macmillan; Frost. (2009).
5. Curtis. (1917). P. 3.
6. Frost. (2009).
7. Edginton, C., DeGraaf, D., Dieser, R., & Edginton, S. (2006). *Leisure and life satisfaction: Foundational perspectives*. New York, NY: McGraw Hill.
8. Louv, R. (2005). *Last child in the woods: Saving our children from nature-deficit disorder*. Chapel Hill, NC: Algonquin Books. P. 99.
9. Rideout, V., Foehr, U., & Roberts, D. (2010). *Generation M²: Media in the lives of 8- to 18-year olds*. Menlo Park, CA: Kaiser Family Foundation.
10. Louv, R. (2005).
11. Clements, R. (2004). An investigation of the status of outdoor play. *Contemporary Issues in Early Childhood, 5*(1), 68–80.
12. Best, J. (2001). *Damned lies and statistics: Untangling numbers from the media, politicians, and activists*. Berkeley: University of California Press; Finkelhor, D., Hammer, H., & Sedlak, A. J. (2002). *Non-family abducted children: National estimates and characteristics*. Washington, DC: Office of Juvenile Justice and Delinquency Prevention, MC19; Louv. (2005).

13. Sutton, A. (2004). Play outside to reduce childhood obesity. *British Medical Journal, 239*, p. 1.

14. Elkind, D. (2006). *The hurried child* (25th anniversary ed.). Cambridge, MA: Da Capo Press; Rosenfeld, A., & Wise, N. (2001). *The over-scheduled child: Avoiding the hyper-parenting trap.* New York, NY: St. Martin's Griffin.

15. Larson, R. W. (2001). How U.S. children and adolescents spend time: What it does (and doesn't) tell us about their development. *Current Directions in Psychological Science, 10,* 160–164; Watts, C. E., & Caldwell, L. L. (2008). Self-determination and free time activity participation as predictors of initiative. *Journal of Leisure Research, 40*(1), 156–181.

16. Larson, R. W., & Seepersad, S. (2003). Adolescents' leisure time in the United States: Partying, sports, and the American experiment. *New Directions for Child and Adolescent Development, 99,* 53-64; Larson, R. W., & Verma, S. (1999). How children and adolescents spend time across the world: Work, play, and developmental opportunities. *Psychological Bulletin, 125*(6), 701–736; McMeeking, D., & Purkayastha, B. (1995). "I can't have my mom running me everywhere": Adolescents, leisure, and accessibility. *Journal of Leisure Research, 27*(4), 360–378.

17. Frost. (2009).

18. Brown, S. & Vaughan, C. (2009). *Play: How it shapes the brain, opens the imagination, and invigorates the soul.* New York, NY: Penguin.

19. Henderson, K. A., & Bialeschki, M. D. (2010). People and nature-based recreation. *Leisure Sciences, 32*(1), 1–2.

20. McKenzie, T. L., & Kahan, D. (2008). Physical activity, public health, and elementary schools. *Elementary School Journal, 108*(3), 171–180; Zygmunt-Fillwalk, E., & Bilello, T. E. (2005). Parents' victory in reclaiming recess for their children. *Childhood Education, 82*(1), 19–24; Robert Wood Johnson Foundation. (2010). *The state of play: Gallup poll of principals on school recess.* Princeton, NJ: Robert Wood Johnson Foundation.

21. Robert Wood Johnson Foundation. (2010). P. 3.

22. Robert Wood Johnson Foundation. (2010).

23. Siedentop, D. (2009). National plan for physical activity: Education sector. *Journal of Physical Activity and Health, 6*(Suppl. 2), S168–S180; No Child Left Inside Act of 2009, H.R. 2054, 111th Cong., 1st Session (2009); No Child Left Inside Act of 2009, S. 866, 111th Congress, 1st Session (2009).

24. Mowen, A., & Baker, B. (2009). Park, recreation, fitness, and sport sector recommendations for a more physically active America: A white paper for the United States National Physical Activity Plan. *Journal of Physical Activity and Health, 6*(Suppl. 2), S236–244.

25. Senauer, A. (2007). *Children and nature network research and studies* (Vol. 2). Albuquerque, NM: Children and Nature Network.

26. Barros, R., Silver, E., & Stein, R. (2009). School recess and group classroom behavior. *Pediatrics, 123*(2), 431–436.

27. Berenson, G. S., Srinivansan, S. R., Bao, W., Newman, W. P., Tracy, R. E., & Wattigney, W. A. (1998). Association between multiple cardiovascular risk factors and atheroslerosis in children and young adults. *New England Journal of Medicine, 338,* 1650–1656; Dwyer, J., Stone, E., Tabg, M., Feldman,

H., Webber, L., Must, A., Perry, C., . . . Parcel, G. (1998). Predictors of over-weight and overfatness in a multiethnic pediatric population. *American Journal of Clinical Nutrition, 67*, 602–610; Maffeis, C., Talamini, G., & Tato, L. (1998). Influence of diet, physical activity and parents' obesity on children' adiposity: A four-year longitudinal study. *International Journal of Obesity, 22*, 758–764.

28. Potwarka, L., Kaczynski, A., & Flack, A. (2008). Places to play: Associa-tion of park space and facilities with healthy weight status among children. *Journal of Community Health, 33*, 344–350.

29. Pelligrini, A. D., & Smith, P. K. (1998). Physical play activity: The nature and function of a neglected aspect of play. *Child Development, 69*, 577–584.

30. Ginsburg, K. (2007). The importance of play in promoting healthy child development and maintaining strong parent-child bonds. *Pediatrics, 119*, 182–191.

31. Walker, S., Chang, S., Powell, C., Simonoff, E., & Grantham-McGregor, S. (2006). Effects of psychological stimulation and dietary supple-mentation in early childhood on psychosocial functioning in late adolescence. *British Medical Journal, 333*(7566), 472.

32. Kuo, F., & Taylor, A. F. (2009). A potential natural treatment for atten-tion-deficit/hyperactivity disorder: Evidence from a national study. *American Journal of Public Health, 94*(9), 1580–1586.

33. Piaget, J. (1962). *Play, dreams and imitation*. New York, NY: Norton; Vygotsky, L. S. (1978). *Mind in society*. Cambridge, MA: Harvard University Press.

34. Ginsburg, K. (2007). The importance of play in promoting healthy child development and maintaining strong parent-child bonds. *Pediatrics, 119*, 182–191.

35. Brown & Vaughan. (2009); Frost, J. L. (1998, June). *Neuroscience, play and brain development*. Paper presented at the IPA/USA Triennial National Conference, Longmont, CO; Shonkoff, J., & Phillips, D. (Eds.). (2000). *Neurons to neighborhoods: The science of early childhood development*. Washington, DC: National Academy Press; Tamis-LeMonda, C. S., Shannon, J. D., Cabrera, N. J., & Lamb, M. E. (2004). Fathers and mothers at play with their 2- and 3-year-olds: Contributions to language and cognitive development. *Child Development, 75*, 1806–1820.

36. Bruce, T. (1999). In praise of inspired and inspiring teachers. In L. Abbott & H. Moylett (Eds.), *Early education transformed* (pp. 33-40). New York, NY: Routledge. P. 40.

37. Bredekamp, S., & Copple, C. (1997). *Developmentally appropriate practice in early childhood programs* (rev. ed.). Washington, DC: National Association for the Education of Young Children.

38. Bedrova, E., & Leong, D. (2003). The importance of being playful. *Educational Leadership, 60*(7), 50–53. P. 51.

39. Barros et al. (2009).

40. Ahsiabi, G. (2007). Play in the preschool classroom: Its socioemotional significance and the teacher's role in play. *Early Childhood Education Journal, 35*(2), 199–207; Bailey, R. (2002). Playing social chess: Children's play and

social intelligence. *Early Years, 22,* 163–173; Hartup, W. (1992). Having friends, making friends, and keeping friends: Relationships as educational contexts. ERIC Digest [Online]. http://ericeece.org/pubs/digests/1992 /hartup92.html; McArdle, P. (2001). Children's play. *Child Care, Health and Development, 27,* 509–514.

41. Smith, P. K., Dalgleish, M., & Herzmark, G. (1981). A comparison of the effects of fantasy play tutoring and skills tutoring in nursery classes. *International Journal of Behavioral Development, 4,* 421–441; Ginsburg. (2007).

42. Piaget. (1962); Vygotsky. (1978); McArdle. (2001); Pelligrini & Smith. (1998).

43. Lindsey, E. W., & Colwell, M. J. (2003). Preschoolers' emotional competence: Links to pretend and physical play. *Child Study Journal, 33,* 39–52.

44. Glover, A. (1999). The role of play in development and learning. In E. Dau (Main Ed.) & E. Jones (Consulting Ed.), *Child's play: Revisiting play in early childhood settings* (pp. 5–15). Baltimore, MD: Paul H. Brookes.

45. Frumkin, H., & Louv, R. (n.d.). Conserving land; Preserving human health. Retrieved from http://www.childrenandnature.org/downloads /frumkinlouv.pdf.

FRAN P. MAINELLA *is a visiting scholar at Clemson University and the sixteenth director of the National Park Service.*

JOEL R. AGATE *is an assistant professor in the Department of Health Education and Recreation at Southern Illinois University Carbondale.*

BRIANNA S. CLARK *is a doctoral student in the Parks, Recreation, and Tourism Management Department at Clemson University.*

Despite operating on the periphery of academic scholarship, adventure-based programs can serve as the prototype for how organized and structured youth development programs should function.

7

Adventure-based programming: Exemplary youth development practice

Jim Sibthorp, Cass Morgan

WHILE READING CONTEMPORARY literature on positive youth development, we have been continually struck by how well the research on youth development aligns with historical practices in adventure-based programs. Despite functioning on the periphery of academic scholarship, theory development, and rigorous science, the better adventure-based programs are at the forefront of professional youth practices. Thus, it seems fitting to advocate for adventure-based programming as a model for positive youth development.

Like any other youth development offering, adventure-based programs vary in structure (short-term experiences, long-term or immersive experiences) and purpose (interpersonal or intrapersonal growth, development of technical skills), offer a range of types of experiences (challenge course, outdoor expeditions), and serve a diversity of populations. These programs also generally share a set of common characteristics, including a novel setting

NEW DIRECTIONS FOR YOUTH DEVELOPMENT, NO. 130, SUMMER 2011 © WILEY PERIODICALS, INC.
Published online in Wiley Online Library (wileyonlinelibrary.com) • DOI: 10.1002/yd.400

and experience, small group sizes, activities involving problem solving and decision making, tasks that are physically and mentally challenging, and an instructor or facilitator who guides participants toward a desired goal.[1] Emerging from a rich history of expedition-style experiences, adventure-based programs have more recently evolved to include shorter formats that share many of the characteristics found in classical expedition-style programs, targeting similar outcomes yet using different modalities. For example, some adventure programs may consist of a one-day challenge course experience and focus on outcomes such as teamwork, communication, and trust. More traditional programs generally last two to four weeks and involve an extended outdoor adventure expedition, where the goal is to promote interpersonal development and intrapersonal growth, and acquire backcountry travel and camping skills.

Extolling the virtues of adventure programs for youth development, Larson states that "adventure programs are not the prototypic structured youth activity."[2] His point is that adventure programs are not the typical model for more common youth programs such as soccer, dance, scouting, or other organized activities and hobbies. While we agree with this premise, we also believe that adventure programs are prototypes of how structured youth programs should function. Although there are clearly differences in adventure programs and other youth activities, many of the qualities of adventure programs can and should be intentionally included in a broader and more accessible spectrum of youth opportunities. Therefore, this article has two primary aims: to explicate the congruency between the current literature on positive youth development and adventure programs and to generalize current tenets of adventure programs to the broader context of youth practice.

Youth development through adventure

There is extensive overlap in developmental theories as to what contributes to well-adjusted youth. Thriving and engaged youth are characterized by six core traits: competence (cognitively and behaviorally), moral character, strong relationships with adults and their peers, a strong sense of identity, empathy, and contributing to self, family, community, and society.[3] This list is consistent with many of the outcomes studied and articulated in the adventure programming literature.

Although lists vary, commonly articulated benefits of adventure programs include perceived competence and self-efficacy, interpersonal skills, identity development, and resilience.[4] In a comprehensive meta-analysis, Hattie and colleagues categorized the major outcomes of adventure programs into academic outcomes, leadership, self-concept, personality, interpersonal outcomes, and adventuresome qualities.[5] Recent research on long-term outcomes from adventure programs includes the ability to function effectively under difficult circumstances, self-confidence, the ability to serve in a leadership role, the ability to work as a team member, and an appreciation of nature.[6] This research indicated that adventure programs may be especially well suited to foster these types of outcomes compared to home, school, work, or sport environments. Although the outcomes of adventure-based programs are generally consistent with the eclectic collection of youth program outcomes, much of the recent research has focused on the important processes and mechanisms that facilitate positive developmental trajectories for youth. Many of these mechanisms from the broader cross-section of youth-related literature are well aligned with what adventure programs provide.

Affording developmental experiences

Much of the recent work on youth development programs has examined what specifically about youth activities and programs best fosters youth development. Although the list is long and the terms vary, some consensus has emerged. It is widely understood that certain activities afford greater developmental experiences to youth. These so-called high-yield activities are goal oriented, require discipline and attention, offer challenge, build skills, and require persistence over time.[7] Another way to consider the mechanisms that support positive development is to look at the contemporary youth program quality measures. The core of these measures typically includes features like peer and adult relationships, physical environment, engagement, productive social norms, skill-building opportunities, routine or structure, and youth leadership.[8]

One of the central models of youth development emphasizes that youth need to feel safe and secure, be given clear structure and expectations that are reasonable, have meaningful and supportive relationships, have a strong sense of belonging, engage in environments that support prosocial behaviors, participate in experiences that allow a sense of empowerment and purpose, and have opportunities to build skills.[9] Research on youth resiliency shows similar indicators with common correlates and predictors to positive outcomes and shows that youth who have caring adults in their life, demonstrate effective problem-solving skills, have prosocial friends, and are served by effective schooling and community services gain important protective mechanisms against unhealthy pathways.[10] In general, there seems to be a consensus that youth need strong relationships with adults or mentors, or both; to have opportunities to build effective life skills; to be goal directed; and to have opportunities for engagement.[11]

Adventure-based programs excel in most of these areas. Supportive relationships, empowerment, structure, and skill building are doctrine for most adventure programs. In a recent study on the National Outdoor Leadership School (NOLS), a global not-for-profit educational institution, Sibthorp, Paisley, and Gookin found that rapport with the adult leaders, supportive groups, and personal empowerment were all related to developmental outcomes for students involved in adventure programming.[12] In addition, traditional models of adventure programming include elements of peer and instructor rapport, challenging tasks requiring skill, and critical reflection and action.[13] Looking specifically at long-term change and growth, a cohort study one to ten years

NEW DIRECTIONS FOR YOUTH DEVELOPMENT • DOI: 10.1002/yd

after participation found that transferable and valuable course outcomes were linked to a variety of mechanisms that ranged from curriculum and educational philosophy to the physical environment and personal triumph.[14] However, instructors were the most frequently reported agents of long-term change. Instructors played critical roles as supportive role models, educators, and sources of inspiration. Other students and group dynamics were also critical catalysts for growth in areas involving self-awareness and the development of capacity for successful teamwork. It is clear that many of the same indicators of high-quality or high-yield youth activities are present in adventure-based programs.

Initiative and engagement

A term that has recently gained traction is Larson's concept of *initiative*. Larson considers initiative a critical outcome for youth, especially because it is considered generative. It may generate or foster additional benefits after the youth leave the program. Larson defines *initiative* as "the ability to be motivated from within to direct attention and effort toward a challenging goal."[15] According to Larson, development of initiative relies on three essential elements: intrinsic motivation, concerted engagement, and a temporal arc. Intrinsic motivation, the most internalized form of motivation, is derived from the inherent interest in and enjoyment of participating in an activity. Concerted engagement involves focused attention and goal-directed concentration. A temporal arc implies that the youth program has a clear beginning, middle, and end and that the end is a goal that will require effort, energy, and perseverance to achieve.

One feature of the work on initiative that is especially well aligned with adventure-based programs is its foundation and association with both the work of Dewey and Csikszentmihalyi regarding optimal experience. According to Dewey, education should strive to be simultaneously goal relevant and enjoyable; he further posits that the combination of enjoyment and goal relevance "defines the ideal mental condition."[16] Although this combination of intrinsic motivation and goal-directed challenge is uncommon in school and unstructured leisure time, it is prevalent in structured voluntary activities, such as hobbies and sports.[17] Recent research on college-age students enrolled in semester-long adventure-based programs supports the premise that such programs are well suited to afford experiences that combine both intrinsic motivation and goal-directed challenge.[18] Such optimally engaging experiences have been linked to both initiative and lifelong learning.[19]

Focus on affording rich, engaging, and potentially developmental experiences for youth is the hallmark of archetypal adventure programs. The research on initiative, self-regulation, and other generative outcomes illustrates a central aspect of what adventure programs can and do provide youth. While adventure and the activity (climbing, hiking, rafting, and sailing, for example) are intrinsically interesting to many youth, the mechanics of a backcountry expedition uniquely position adventure-based programs to supply an abundance of experiences that are authentically goal relevant, engaging, and challenging to participants.

Developmental systems theory

Systems theory is another approach to youth development that is well suited to adventure programming. Within this framework, development does not occur in a vacuum. Rather, it is a mutual product of biological characteristics intersecting with the daily experiences and settings in which youth live. Development emerges through an individual-context exchange embedded within a multilevel (psychological, biological, cultural, historical, and social) system.[20] Such a dynamic system points to a process where an individual is both being shaped by biological and contextual factors and facilitating and driving his or her own development.[21] This dynamic system requires a young person to make continuous adjustments within various interactions, circumstances, and environments that depend on the ability to adapt cognitively, physically, behaviorally, and socioemotionally.[22] In fact, the social interactions and social understandings within youth's lives directly influence the development of cognitive competence and the ability to adapt to one's environment and achieve positive outcomes.[23] Such adaptive efforts present a number of challenges to youth who are still undergoing maturational changes that may make accessing the necessary resources to adjust successfully difficult. Subsequently, context becomes an important element when identifying environmental nutriments necessary to foster engaged and thriving youth.[24]

Adventure-based programs have been considered microcosms for personal growth and development.[25] The remoteness and small group interdependence of these programs makes the contextually relevant systems much more manageable from both the participant and adult leader perspectives. When a participant, for example, fails to manage conflict, do her fair share, or show up on time, the ripple effects on the other features of the system readily manifest themselves. Participants realize that their behaviors have consequences for others and that the group's performance is directly tied to individual action or inaction. This type of isolation and disconnection from larger and more powerful systems of influence in youths' lives is both a strength and a weakness of many adventure-based programs.

Features of adventure-based programs

While adventure-based programs have much in common with more traditional youth development programs, including their nature, mechanics, and outcomes, they are also markedly different. Remoteness, density, and the physical environment in which the programs operate are obvious differences. The intentional targeting of holistic outcomes, the social experience, and program novelty are notable features as well.

One area where adventure programs do not align well with the current literature on positive youth development is connecting the program with families and communities. This type of connection is typically reliant on community and family interaction, which is difficult in most traditional adventure programs. However, in exchange for this lack of connection, adventure programs offer remoteness and autonomy.

Expedition groups, common in typical adventure-based programs, largely function as interdependent autonomous units. They are unplugged and disconnected from external influences. Expeditions inherently involve planning, goal setting, communication, and leadership, and they embody teamwork and personal responsibility. Unlike more integrated experiences, where, for example, a group of adolescents might design, plan, and implement a day camp for children, both planners and participants are the same.[26] This affords adult leaders additional freedom that is not always present when working with external parties—the ability to fail. Despite the inherent learning that might come from failure, having to explain to disappointed children and angry parents that the planned community "day camp" was canceled due to poor adolescent leadership is untenable. In contrast, hardly any explanation is necessary when a planned route is not manageable for an expedition group. The learning is real, raw, authentic, and experiential. The reflection, processing, and discussion, if even necessary, are also immediately relevant. Because the group is self-contained, isolated, and neither dependent on nor responsible to another party, the "failure" is easily redressed through the next day's plan, and the flexibility of the remote nature and independence becomes a powerful educational tool.

Another difference is the density and intensity. Very few other youth programs can match the intensity of an adventure education experience. Consider the time involved in a thirty-day expedition typical at NOLS. Assuming sixteen-hour days, this month-long course entails almost five hundred hours of immersive content. Minimal math quickly illustrates that this single month matches several years of seasonal sports participation. The intensity of adventure programs is often magnified by their compression into discrete blocks of time. This level of program density is uncommon in most other structured youth programs.

Adventure programs typically leverage the authentic power and educational potential of the physical environment. The environments, be they a lengthy section of rugged alpine terrain or a gymnasium floor developed into an obstacle course, are critical to the developmental process. These environments afford opportunities for engagement, learning, emotional highs and lows, and, ultimately, meaningful experiences. While many environments might be shaped to afford an adventure experience, the qualities of the physical spaces are viewed by adventure educators as a critical aspect of the adventure experience.

Adventure programs have never avoided intentionality and explicitly targeting holistic, value-laden, and amorphous outcomes. Such outcomes are often internalized best through holistic, visceral, and sensorial immersion in the content. For example, a participant who goes to NOLS will be exposed to its leadership curriculum, will participate as a leader of the day several times during the course, will be debriefed by both peers and the course leaders on his or her performance with an eye toward improvement, and will be given a course grade on leadership. One of the course leaders then personally discusses the course grade with the participant. He or she learns about how to function and behave as a leader by watching peers, watching course leaders, trying to lead, feedback from others, and, ultimately, by reflecting on his or her own successes and failures. Leadership is experienced and learned in a comprehensive, incremental, and sensorial context where leadership is an authentic need. Such intentionality and focus on outcomes not explicitly addressed in most school systems allow more targeted development in areas that other programs neglect.

The social experience is also different from more typical youth settings. Smaller groups that are together for extended periods of time, often with multiple adult role models, afford certain supports and opportunities not present in all youth recreation settings. Cliques are less common because intragroup cooperation is typically necessary for group success. Adult leaders are able to monitor and influence the groups' social structure, actively assisting productive and positive social norms to develop. Smith, Steel, and Gidlow posit that the social nature of these temporary (several weeks in length) communities is part of what makes them different, and thus powerful.[27] Their temporary nature allows and encourages youth to explore different behaviors and roles. Shaffer terms this the "looking glass self" and explains how during identity formation, youth benefit from testing different behaviors and identity types and observing how others react to these alternate identity explorations.[28] Ultimately the unique, yet temporary, nature of a small group expedition affords some potent features. The intense nature of these experiences can accelerate group development or group destruction and provides participants an opportunity to live and experiment in a microcosm that may not directly affect their other lives.

While many experiences for youth are unfamiliar, adventure programs often provide novel experiences that can quickly draw and hold the attention of youth. The novelty of these experiences is often considered an equalizer that erodes preexisting power structures.[29] In other words, traditional skills and abilities may be of little use on a backcountry expedition, and previously unfamiliar skills such as navigation or knot tying have immediate relevance. The natural appeal of novelty and risk taking for many young people can be powerful mechanisms in youth programs. As adolescents are drawn to these novel and risky behaviors,[30] offering young people developmentally appropriate and constructive ways to engage in risk recreation may be engaging and even developmental.[31]

While the adventure modality may serve as a powerful developmental tool, it is also inaccessible in its traditional form. Constrained by time, money, interest, social influence, and physical proximity, many youth will never embark on an extended backcountry adventure experience where they are immersed in nature with a small group of peers. To address this obvious disconnect, some programs are trying to make adventure modalities more accessible to youth. Project Adventure, for example, offers training to educators who wish to incorporate the use of adventure activities and techniques into their schools and classrooms. The idea is to integrate the best practices of the adventure modality with the content and context of K-12 schooling. Because of the inherent benefits to students, these programs are becoming increasingly popular with physical education teachers. Another example is Outward Bound's move to more urban centers and expeditionary learning schools. Both of these initiatives represent a strategic decision to move the successful Outward Bound process closer to populations that might otherwise find this programming inaccessible.

Although there are many differences between a two-week backpacking expedition and playing in a youth basketball league, there are also some similarities, especially as they apply to affording positive and constructive opportunities for youth. Adventure programming does some things extremely well, and these lessons should be considered by a wider swath of practitioners working with youth. Intentionally targeting more holistic growth and attending to the social experience of the youth remain critical factors for positive youth development. Furthermore, in considering the power of autonomy, intensity, novelty, and the physical environment, traditional structured youth programs might learn from adventure-based program practices.

Conclusion

Youth have long been the focus of adventure programs. While often forgotten, neglected, and marginalized in the research literature because of their narrow foci, exemplary adventure programs for youth have long flourished. Kurt Hahn, one of the founders of Outward Bound, shaped his educational philosophy from years working with young men at progressive boarding schools in Germany and England. His holistic educational philosophy is consistent with much of the research on quality youth programming today. Examples of peer leadership, scaffolding, autonomy, authenticity, and engagement are central in Hahn's practices.[32] Thus, while not prototypical in some ways, many adventure programs are prototypical in others: small groups, invested leaders, challenging activities, skill building, temporal arcs, planning and goal setting, and so forth. These are core elements of the historical and philosophical roots of contemporary adventure-based practices.

In addition to their potential as exemplary program models, an emerging body of literature further recognizes that discrete experiences can be extremely powerful agents of development and change. Referred to as developmental cascades, discrete, high-quality experiences may afford people incremental development that can be stitched together over their lives.[33] Through repeated exposure to these discrete yet developmentally rich experiences, researchers are now able to see how personal and contextual variables intersect and transact across the life span to predict healthy trajectories.[34]

This notion of developmental cascades reinforces the premise that even while limited in time and space, adventure programs can be important catalysts for growth and change. Adventure programs can create microcosms that simplify the larger sociocultural context and allow youth to engage in authentic experiences where they develop important life skills and learn how to practice adaptive negotiations through challenging situations. Adventure programs excel at providing opportunities for youth to engage in healthy relationship building, feel acceptance, and develop socioemotional competence—assets that are particularly powerful in promoting positive outcomes and disrupting negative outcomes.[35] It is time to recognize the important role that adventure programs play for many youth and to embrace what these diverse and successful programs can teach the general field of positive youth development.

Notes

1. Hattie, J., Marsh, H. W., Neill, J. T., & Richards, G. E. (1997). Adventure education and Outward Bound: Out-of-class experiences that have a lasting effect. *Review of Educational Research, 67*, 43–87.

2. Larson, R. (2000). Towards a psychology of positive youth development. *American Psychologist, 55*, 170–183.

3. Lerner, R., Brentano, C., Dowling, E., & Anderson, P. (2002). *Positive youth development: Thriving as the basis of personhood and civil society*. In R. Lerner, C. Taylor, & A. von Eye (Eds.), *Pathways to positive development among diverse youth. New Directions for Youth Development, 95*, 149–164. San Francisco, CA:

Jossey-Bass; Roth, J., & Brooks-Gunn, J. (2003). Youth development programs: Risk, prevention and policy. *Journal of Adolescent Health, 32*, 170–182.

4. Sibthorp, J. (2003a). An empirical look at Walsh and Golins' adventure education process model: Relationships between antecedent factors, perceptions of characteristics of an adventure education experience, and changes in self-efficacy. *Journal of Leisure Research, 35*(1), 80–106; Moote, G., & Wodarski, J. (1997). The acquisition of life-skills through adventure-based activities and programs: A review of the literature. *Adolescence, 32*(1), 143–168; Sammet, K. (2010). Relationships matter: Adolescent girls and relational development in adventure education. *Journal of Experiential Education, 33*(2), 151–165; Duerden, M. D., Widmer, M. A., Taniguchi, S., & McCoy, J. K. (2009). Adventures in identity development: The impact of a two-week adventure program on adolescent identity development. *Identity: An International Journal of Theory and Research, 9*(4), 341–359; Green, G., Kleiber, D., & Tarrant, M. (2000). The effect of an adventure-based recreation program on development of resiliency in low-income minority youth. *Journal of Park and Recreation Administration, 18*, 76–97; Neill, J., & Dias, K. (2001). Adventure education and resilience: The double-edged sword. *Journal of Adventure Education and Outdoor Learning, 1*(2), 35–42.

5. Hattie et al. (1997).

6. Sibthorp, J., Paisley, K., Furman, N., & Gookin, J. (2008). Long-term impacts attributed to participation in adventure education: Preliminary findings from NOLS. *Research in Outdoor Education, 9*, 86–102.

7. Caldwell, L. (2005). Recreation and youth development. In P. Witt & L. Caldwell (Eds.), *Recreation and youth development* (pp. 169–191). State College, PA: Venture Publishing.

8. Yohalem, N., & Wilson-Ahlstrom, A. (2010). Inside the black box: Assessing and improving quality in youth programs. *American Journal of Community Psychology, 45*(3/4), 350–357.

9. Eccles, J., & Gootman, J. (2002). *Community programs to promote youth development.* Washington, DC: Committee on Community-Level Programs for Youth, Board on Children, Youth, and Families, Commission on Behavioral and Social Sciences Education, National Research Council and Institute of Medicine.

10. Masten, A. (2004). Regulatory processes, risk, and resilience in adolescent development. *Annals of the New York Academy of Sciences, 1021*, 310–319.

11. Pittman, K., Irby, M., Tolman, J., Yohalem, N., & Ferber, T. (2003). *Preventing problems, promoting development, encouraging engagement: Competing priorities or inseparable goals?* Washington, DC: Forum for Youth Investment.

12. Sibthorp, J., Paisley, K., & Gookin, J. (2007). Exploring participant development through adventure-based recreation programming: A model from the National Outdoor Leadership School. *Leisure Sciences, 29*(1), 1–18.

13. Gager, R. (1977). Experiential learning process flow. *Journal of Experiential Education, 1*, 4–5; Walsh, V., & Golins, G. (1976). *The exploration of the Outward Bound process.* Denver: Colorado Outward Bound School.

14. Sibthorp, J., Furman, N., Paisley, K., Schumann, S., & Gookin, J. (2011). Mechanisms of learning transfer in adventure education: Qualitative results from the NOLS transfer survey. *Journal of Experiential Education*, *34*(2).

15. Larson. (2000)

16. Dewey, J. (1910/1991). *How we think*. Amherst, NY: Prometheus Books.

17. Csikszentmihalyi, M., & Larson, R. (1984). *Being adolescent: Conflict and growth in the teenage years*. New York: Basic Books; Larson. (2000).

18. Sibthorp, J., Schumann, S., Gookin, J., Baynes, S., Paisley, K., & Rathunde, K. (2011). Experiential education and lifelong learning: Examining optimal engagement in college students. [Abstract] *Journal of Experiential Education*, *33*(4), 388–392.

19. Larson. (2000); Rathunde, K. (2009). Experiential wisdom and optimal experience: Interviews with three distinguished lifelong learners. *Journal of Adult Development*, *17*(2), 81–93.

20. Gestsdottir, S., & Lerner, R. (2008). Positive development in adolescence: The development and role of intentional self-regulation. *Human Development*, *51*, 202–224.

21. Brandtstadter, J. (2006). Action perspectives on human development. In R. M. Lerner & W. Damon (Eds.), *Theoretical models of human development: Vol. 1. Handbook of child psychology* (6th ed., pp. 516–568). Hoboken, NJ: Wiley.

22. Lerner, R. (2002). *Concepts and theories of human development* (3rd ed.). Mahwah, NJ: Erlbaum.

23. Lewin-Bizan, S., Bowers, E., & Lerner, R. (2010). One good thing leads to another: Cascades of positive youth development among American adolescents. *Development and Psychopathology*, *22*, 759–770; Lewis, C., Koyasu, M., Oh, S., Ogawa, A., Short, B., & Huang, Z. (2009). Culture, executive function, and social understanding. *New Directions for Child and Adolescent Development*, *123*, 69–85. San Francisco, CA: Jossey-Bass.

24. Lerner et al. (2002).

25. Sibthorp, J. (2003b). Learning transferable skills through adventure education: The role of an authentic process. *Journal of Adventure Education and Outdoor Learning*, *3*(2), 145–157; Brown, M. (2010). Transfer: Outdoor adventure education's Achilles heel? Changing participation as a viable option. *Australian Journal of Outdoor Education*, *14*(1), 13–22.

26. Larson, R., Hansen, D., & Walker, K. (2005). Everybody's gotta give: Development of initiative and teamwork within a youth program. In J. L. Mahoney, R. W. Larson, & J. S. Eccles (Eds.), *Organized activities as contexts of development: Extracurricular activities, after-school and community programs* (pp. 159–183). Mahwah, NJ: Erlbaum.

27. Smith, E., Steel, G., & Gidlow, B. (2010). The temporary community: Student experiences of school-based outdoor education programmes. *Journal of Experiential Education*, *33*(2), 136–150.

28. Shaffer, L. S. (2005). From mirror self-recognition to the looking glass self: Exploring the justification hypothesis. *Journal of Clinical Psychology*, *61*(1), 47–65.

29. Garst, B., Scheider, I., & Baker, D. (2001). Outdoor adventure program participation impacts on adolescent self-perception. *Journal of Experiential Education, 24*(1), 41.

30. Steinberg, L. (2007). Risk taking in adolescence. *Current Directions in Psychological Science, 16*(2), 55–59.

31. Dayan, J., Bernard, A., Olliac, B., Mailhes, A., & Kermarrec, S. (2010). Adolescent brain development, risk-taking and vulnerability to addiction. *Journal of Physiology-Paris, 104,* 279-286; D'Silva, M., Harrington, N., Palmgreen, P., Donohew, L., & Lorch, E. (2001). Drug use prevention for the high sensation seeker: The role of alternative activities. *Substance Use and Misuse, 36*(3), 375–385.

32. Miner, J., & Boldt, J. (1981). *Outward Bound USA: Learning through experience in adventure-based education.* New York: Morrow; Skidelsky, R. (1969). *English progressive schools.* Baltimore, MD: Penguin.

33. Masten, A., & Cicchetti, D. (2010). Developmental cascades. *Development and Psychopathology, 22,* 491–495.

34. Masten, A. S., Roisman, G. I., Long, J. D., Burt, K. B., Obradović, J., Riley, J. R., & ... Tellegen, A. (2005). Developmental cascades: Linking academic achievement and externalizing and internalizing symptoms over 20 years. *Developmental Psychology, 41,* 733–746.

35. Lewin-Bizan et al. (2010).

JIM SIBTHORP *is an associate professor in the Department of Parks, Recreation, and Tourism at the University of Utah.*

CASS MORGAN *is a doctoral candidate in the Department of Parks, Recreation, and Tourism at the University of Utah.*

Youth are often the primary group for parks and recreation organizations, yet recreation professionals are often not adequately prepared in the principles and practices of youth development. Similarly, youth workers outside the recreation field often lack information on basic recreation program design and activity leadership.

8

A competency-based approach to preparing staff as recreation and youth development leaders

Robert J. Barcelona, Amy R. Hurd, Jennifer A. Bruggeman

AS OTHERS HAVE NOTED throughout this issue, leisure-time activities have the potential to foster a wide range of positive developmental outcomes for youth. However, these outcomes do not accrue to youth by mere participation in recreational activities. In fact, a strong argument can be made that poorly framed and delivered activities may not have much, if any, beneficial effect and can even undermine positive outcomes. To put it simply, the context and setting where recreation activities happen matter, and the adults who plan and lead these activities often have a significant impact on whether participation yields positive developmental outcomes.

NEW DIRECTIONS FOR YOUTH DEVELOPMENT, NO. 130, SUMMER 2011 © WILEY PERIODICALS, INC.
Published online in Wiley Online Library (wileyonlinelibrary.com) • DOI: 10.1002/yd.401

Researchers in the broader youth development field have noted the critical importance of nonparental adults in the lives of youth.[1] The leisure studies literature has also addressed the need for trained and competent staff and volunteers to work with youth in a variety of recreation program contexts and settings.[2] Yet discussion related to the lack of adequate preparation for youth workers in a variety of settings, including leisure services, has been noted in the literature.[3] This is perhaps best summed up by a parks and recreation director who commented on the need for developing partnerships with colleges and universities to better prepare her staff: "Too often, recreation is seen as a soft environment where they can put anyone. After all, what skills does it take to open the gym doors and throw out a couple of basketballs? Practitioners and educators need to work together to raise awareness and change these kinds of perceptions."[4]

Youth development is about more than just occupying time, opening the gym doors, and rolling out the basketballs. Others have noted the competency gap that exists between youth workers "with energy and good intentions but little training or knowledge of child and youth development."[5] This is especially prevalent in the area of leisure services, where frontline recreation staff members are hired primarily based on their skills and abilities to lead specific recreation-oriented activities. This competency gap may be exacerbated by the nature of frontline staff positions in leisure services settings. While some frontline staff positions are filled by full-time professionals with an academic background in parks, recreation, leisure studies, or related fields, many are filled with part-time or seasonal staff members with varying professional and academic backgrounds. In addition, leisure services providers heavily use volunteers, who play a critical role in the delivery of recreation programs and services. Full-time program-level staff in recreation organizations may be highly competent in leisure services delivery, including program planning, activity leadership, and evaluation but they may not have a broad understanding of youth development principles and practices.

Recreational activities are also offered within youth development organizations that would not identify themselves as part of the leisure services field. Full-service youth development organizations such as Boys and Girls Clubs, after-school programs, and 4-H use recreational activities as programming areas within their overall program. Because entry- and program-level staff members in these organizations are not likely hired based on their competence in recreation program delivery, they may lack expertise in choosing, designing, leading, and evaluating recreation activities. The result can be the provision of low-yield activities that do not maximize positive developmental outcomes or meet program goals. For example, teachers who are tasked with leading physical activities are less likely to implement developmentally appropriate programs within their classrooms or schools when they lack proper training in activity leadership.[6] Improving access to educational programs focusing on youth development and recreation, as well as providing continuous training and development opportunities for recreation leaders in youth-serving organizations, can help to close the competency gaps frequently noted in the literature.

A developmental model for recreation delivery

One of the challenges in understanding staff development issues is the complexity in how recreation activities are employed within youth-serving organizations. Table 8.1 depicts a conceptual model for understanding how recreation programming efforts can move from an activity-centered focus to a more youth-centered approach. Staff development efforts can start with helping youth workers move beyond activity-centered approaches that focus on a narrow range of outcomes toward a more youth-centered approach. Youth-centered approaches view recreation activities as modalities for delivering a broad set of positive developmental outcomes and seek to engage and involve youth in the process. At the same time, they focus on strengthening and building developmental assets through intentional and purposeful program planning.

Table 8.1. A developmental model of recreation delivery

Activity centered		Youth centered	
Diversion	Activity focus	Activity-outcome focus	Outcome focus
Focus: Occupying time	Focus: Building activity-specific competence	Focus: Achieving developmental outcomes through specific recreational activities	Focus: Achieving developmental outcomes through different recreational activities
Examples: Low-yield activities such as movies and video games, open gyms, free play	Examples: Youth sports, art programs	Examples: The First Tee, Girls on the Run	Examples: Outdoor adventure activities, summer camp programs

Activity-centered approaches

Activity-centered approaches to providing recreational activities are common in many youth-serving programs. While young people may find these activities to be engaging and fun, their developmental potential may be limited by the lack of purpose and intentionality in program design:

- *Diversionary activity.* Diversionary activities—open gyms, movies, video games, or other types of low-yield activities—are used primarily as a means to occupy time. Staff may employ a minimum level of planning, structure, and supervision, but activities are generally not chosen for any particular purpose outside of occupying time or providing safe spaces and places to play.
- *Activity focused.* The primary objective is on leading or teaching a particular recreation activity, with a focus on developing activity-specific outcomes. Outcomes might include program-focused indicators such as increased participation levels, or they might include individual outcomes such as increasing task-specific competence, activity-related self-efficacy, or physical fitness. Activity-focused programs might include agency-sponsored youth sport programs or instruction-centered

activities such as swimming lessons. Staff in these programs are usually highly competent in leading their particular activity (for example, swim instructors, youth sport coaches), but may lack specific training or education in youth development or in understanding the connections between specific program interventions and corresponding developmental outcomes.

Youth-centered approaches

Programs that use a youth-centered approach focus on the developmental potential that recreation activities hold. This approach intentionally seeks to maximize choice, voice, and the developmental assets that accrue through participation in meaningful and engaging recreation experiences. The eight features of positive youth development settings outlined by the National Research Council-Institute of Medicine can be used as a guide to help recreation leaders create positive developmental contexts: ensuring that programs are physically and psychologically safe; providing programs with appropriate boundaries and structure; facilitating supportive relationships between youth and staff; providing opportunities for youth to belong; promoting positive social norms; providing support for efficacy and mattering; providing opportunities for skill building; and integrating school, family, and neighborhood efforts.[7] Although not all of these eight features will be incorporated into every recreation program or activity, they are a useful set of guidelines for helping staff reframe their programs and activity contexts. The following are examples of youth-centered approaches to recreation program or activity delivery:

- *Activity-outcome focus.* The activity-outcome approach uses specific recreation activities or modalities to maximize developmental assets. Recreation leaders conceptualize the outcomes that they want to deliver prior to program delivery and intentionally plan program interventions accordingly. Program outcomes go beyond those that are typically associated with the specific activity (for example, becoming a more competent swimmer, increasing daily physical activity). Examples include programs such as the First Tee, which uses golf as a means for teaching life skills, and Girls on the Run, which uses running as a means for having an impact on a broad range of developmental outcomes for preteen girls, including self-concept and healthy lifestyle choices.[8]

• *Outcome focus.* The outcome focus approach recognizes recreation programs as containers that hold the potential for a variety of developmental experiences; specific activities like running, basketball, or music are important in that they help to engage participants and achieve developmental goals. While the activity-outcome focus seeks to maximize the developmental potential of a specific recreation activity through intentional program design and planning, the outcome focus starts with a desired set of outcomes in mind and chooses activities that are best suited to delivering those outcomes. This can be done in consultation with young people themselves, maximizing both youth choice and voice within the process of program planning. Examples of outcome-focused programs and activities are outdoor education experiences, teen center programming, and comprehensive summer camp programs.

The critical role that youth workers play in the lives of young people makes training and staff development a key component in building positive youth development settings. The leisure services industry has a long history of providing programs and activities for youth and has developed a clear set of pathways for building competence in recreation management and programming, including accredited academic preparation programs, professional certification, continuing education opportunities, and staff and volunteer training. However, it is unclear whether recreation leaders are adequately prepared in the work of youth development. Luckily, a considerable amount of work has been done outside the recreation field to differentiate "youth work" from "youth development" and to articulate a set of core competencies for youth development workers. We discuss some of this work next, with a particular emphasis on how the recreation field can begin to draw on this body of knowledge to strengthen training and professional development for staff working with youth-serving programs.

Competencies in youth development and recreation

Competencies refer to the skills, knowledge, abilities, and characteristics needed to be successful in a job. More precisely related to the field of youth development, competencies are the "knowledge, skills and personal attributes workers need to create and support positive youth development settings."[9] There is ongoing debate about the best methods for obtaining professional competencies in both the youth development and recreation fields. While the debate is often framed as more education versus more experience, most experts have recognized that the answer lies somewhere in the middle. Ultimately what will close the competency gap is a combination of education- and experience-based approaches.

Youth development competencies

Numerous efforts have been made to identify the core competencies of youth workers over the past decade. Much of the early work on youth development competencies was focused on the executive level, while recent work in this area has focused on the needs of frontline youth workers.[10] One of the most recent documents is *Youth Development Worker Competencies*, developed by the National Collaboration for Youth, in partnership with a range of on-the-ground youth development organizations, which sets out ten competencies:

1. Understands and applies basic child and adolescent development principles
2. Communicates and develops positive relationships with youth
3. Adapts, facilitates, and evaluates age-appropriate activities with and for the group
4. Respects and honors cultural and human diversity
5. Involves and empowers youth

6. Identifies potential risk factors and takes measures to reduce those risks
7. Cares for, involves, and works with families and communities
8. Works as part of a team and shows professionalism
9. Demonstrates the attributes and qualities of a positive role model
10. Interacts with and relates to youth in ways that support asset building

These entry-level competencies place a heavy premium on face-to-face youth work and direct service delivery, while recognizing the importance of relationships, diversity, and developmental ecologies and systems. It has been suggested that this list of ten competencies, along with their thirty-two competency indicators, can be used in the professional development of youth workers by identifying potential competency gaps, building academic curricula, developing training or staff development initiatives, or developing certification or credentialing programs.[11]

Recreation competencies

The field of parks, recreation, and leisure services has had a long history of addressing professional development issues through the development of competency models. Research on the competencies of leisure services staff has been conducted in the public, non-profit, and commercial sectors; within specialization areas in the field, such as recreational sports; and within various staffing levels within specific organizations, such as entry level, executive level, and board members.[12] Although youth-specific programs and activities are some of the most popular program offerings in the leisure services industry, little or no research has focused on the specific competencies of youth workers within recreation and leisure services settings.

While research on competencies has been conducted and established in a wide range of areas within the leisure services field, the profession has also identified a set of core competencies that likely cuts across the various and diverse sectors, specializations, and organizational types. Core competencies in recreation are outlined and identified by the Council on Accreditation of Parks, Recreation, Tourism, and Related Professions. They form the basis for accrediting undergraduate academic programs in recreation and leisure studies and for professional certification in the field (the Certified Park and Recreation Professional credential).

Academic accreditation standards for recreation and leisure studies curricula encompass a range of benchmarks, including setting minimum standards for administration, faculty, and instructional resources, yet at the heart of the program are the 8.0 standards which focus on the core competencies of entry-level recreation staff. [13] Core competencies in recreation tend to be focused on leadership, management, programming, and administration and focus on the developmental needs of humans across the life span; they are outlined in the left-hand column of Table 8.2.

Table 8.2. A side-by-side comparison of competencies in recreation and youth development

Council on accreditation competencies (8.0 Series)	National Collaboration for Youth competencies for youth development workers
Conceptual foundations	
Understanding of the conceptual foundations of play, recreation, and leisure	
Understanding of the significance of play, recreation, and leisure in contemporary society	
Understanding of the significance of play, recreation, and leisure throughout the life span	Understands basic child and adolescent development principles
Understanding of the interrelationship between leisure behavior and the natural environment	
Understanding environmental ethics and its relationship to leisure behavior	
Profession	
Understanding of the following as they relate to recreation, park resources, and leisure services: history, professional organizations, current issues and trends, ethical principles and professionalism, professional competence and resources for professional development	Understands basic child and adolescent development principles Works as part of a team and shows professionalism *(Continued)*

NEW DIRECTIONS FOR YOUTH DEVELOPMENT • DOI: 10.1002/yd

Table 8.2. (*Continued*)

Council on accreditation competencies (8.0 Series)	National Collaboration for Youth competencies for youth development workers
Delivery system	
Understanding the roles, interrelationships, and use of diverse delivery systems addressing recreation, park resources, and leisure	Cares for, involves, and works with families and communities
Understanding of the importance of leisure service delivery systems for diverse populations	Respects and honors cultural diversity
Understanding inclusive practices as they apply to operating programs and services and design of areas and facilities	Respects and honors cultural diversity
Understanding of the roles, interrelationships, and use of diverse leisure delivery systems in promoting community development and economic development	Cares for, involves, and works with families and communities
Program and event planning	
Understanding of the variety of programs and services to enhance individual, group, and community quality of life	
Ability to implement the following principles and procedures related to program and event planning for individual, group, and community quality of life: assessment of needs; development of outcome-oriented goals and objectives; selection and coordination of programs, events, and resources; marketing of programs and events; preparation, operation, and maintenance of venues; implementation of programs and events; evaluation of programs and events	Interacts with and relates to youth in ways that support asset building
Understanding of group dynamics and processes	Adapts, facilitates, and evaluates age-appropriate activities with and for the group
Ability to use various leadership techniques to enhance individual, group, and community experiences	
Administration and management	
Ability to apply basic principles of research and data analysis related to recreation, park resources, and leisure services	
Understanding of the fundamental principles and procedures of management	
Understanding of the principles and procedures of human resource management	

Table 8.2. (*Continued*)

Council on accreditation competencies (8.0 Series)	National Collaboration for Youth competencies for youth development workers
Understanding of the principles and procedures of supervisory leadership	
Understanding of the principles and procedures of budgeting and financial management	
Understanding of the principles and procedures related to agency marketing techniques and strategies	
Ability to use the tools of professional communication	
Ability to apply current technology to professional practice	
Knowledge of the following principles and procedures of developing areas and facilities: assessment, planning, functional design, evaluation, operation and maintenance	
Legal aspects	
Understanding of the following related to recreation, park resources, and leisure services: legal foundations and the legislative process, contracts and tort law, regulatory agents and methods of compliance	
Understanding of the principles and practices of safety, emergency, and risk management related to recreation, park resources, and leisure services	Identifies potential risk factors (in a program environment) and takes measures to reduce those risks

However, given the diverse staffing patterns of recreation and leisure services agencies, there is no guarantee that all staff members will have been exposed to the content embedded in all of these areas. This is particularly true for both full- and part-time (or volunteer) staff members coming from academic preparation programs outside of studies or for those without college or university course work.

Implications for practice

There are a number of areas of similarity and overlap between the core competencies outlined for entry-level staff members working in both youth development and recreation settings, as well as some potential gaps (see Table 8.2). Both sets of competencies focus on areas such as diversity, risk management, professionalism, human development, group processes, and the larger ecologies that have an impact on youth. However, there are notable differences between the two competency models as well, and youth workers who provide recreation activities can benefit from exposure to both sets of core competencies.

Although most leisure services organizations devote a significant amount of their programming efforts to serving youth, many are intergenerational in scope and have a mandate to serve participants over a wide range of ages and abilities. Academic preparation programs in parks and recreation have taken this into account, and university courses in human development are often broad and taught from a life span perspective. Staff working with youth in leisure services organizations may not be exposed to the specific principles and practices of youth development. Because of this, recreation staff could benefit from exposure to the competencies of entry-level youth workers. This exposure can come from a variety of sources, including academic preparation programs in youth development, continuing education opportunities, and staff training. In addition to the recreation-specific competencies already outlined, recreation staff can supplement their existing knowledge with the following youth development competencies:

- Understanding the concept of positive youth development and asset building
- Ability to implement a youth-centered approach for recreation program delivery
- Knowledge of youth risk factors and ability to identify potential areas of risk for youth
- Understanding the importance of youth involvement and ability to implement youth voice within the scope of recreation activity programming
- Understanding principles of child and adolescent development principles

• Ability to effectively communicate and build relationships with youth

At the same time, staff providing recreation activities for youth outside the leisure services field may not have exposure to the recreation-specific competencies outlined in the core competencies of recreation staff. While the core competencies of entry-level youth workers understandably place a heavy premium on face-to-face interactions with youth, youth workers may need to supplement their knowledge base with content related to recreation program planning, activity leadership, and administrative practice. In addition to the competencies of entry-level youth workers, the following recreation-related competencies may also be important:

• Understanding the conceptual and theoretical bases underlying leisure, recreation, and play
• Ability to implement a youth-centered approach for recreation program delivery
• Ability to plan, design, implement, and evaluate intentional and purposeful recreation programs
• Knowledge of recreation activity leadership and ability to lead specific activities effectively
• Understanding the technical aspects of legality and risk management in recreation
• Knowledge of effective management and administrative practices, including program marketing, fiscal management, and human resources

From the field

Like the field of youth development, there are multiple paths to careers in the recreation industry, and staff often come from diverse academic backgrounds. This is particularly true when one considers the varied experiences and backgrounds of the volunteers who deliver recreation services to youth in their communities. However, the field of recreation and leisure studies has developed a delivery system for professional development, focused on accredited academic preparation programs that include experiential learning through field-based internships, a national certification program for park and recreation professionals, and continuing education opportunities offered through a network of associations designed to meet the needs of working professionals.

In addition, organizations such as the National Recreation and Park Association (NRPA) and the American Camp Association (ACA) have established agency accreditation programs that enable recreation organizations to demonstrate their commitment to national standards of best practices. For example, the NRPA program has established best practices in areas such as programs and services management, planning, administration, and human resource management. The human resource management section dictates that agencies offer in-service training, employee development, and succession planning. Succession planning requires that agencies assess current competencies of employees and future competency needs of the agency and develop plans to close any competency gaps.

This multilayered system of professional development for recreation workers is designed to accommodate specialty areas of the field, such as aquatics, fitness, playgrounds, and park management. However, this existing professional development delivery system of academic preparation, certification, continuing education opportunities, and agency-specific training can do more to better prepare recreation staff to work with youth. We discuss some of these ways that the field is incorporating youth development into these areas in the next sections.

Academic preparation

Because youth development is an emerging priority for the recreation field, recreation and leisure studies curricula can and should do more to incorporate youth development competencies into existing academic programs, course work, and field-based learning experiences. For example, the University of New Hampshire's undergraduate interdisciplinary minor in adolescent and youth development is a collaborative effort between a number of academic preparation programs, including recreation management, family studies, education, and kinesiology. In addition to core course work in youth development principles and practices, students can take courses in recreation activity leadership, programming, and sports coaching.[14]

A growing number of graduate-level youth development academic programs offer course work, certificate, and degree options for professionals with baccalaureate degrees. These programs are offered through a variety of delivery systems, including on-campus, online, and blended course formats. For example, Clemson University offers a fully online master's degree and graduate-level certificate program in youth development leadership. The program is designed to meet the needs of working professionals in the youth development and recreation fields, is flexible in approach, and encourages collaboration and networking by having students progress through the program as a cohort. Courses are delivered both asynchronously and in real time using Web-based conferencing technologies. Online and distance education programs that provide opportunities for collaborative learning offer real promise for academic preparation in youth development. This is particularly important because research has shown that youth workers value opportunities to share their experiences and learn from one another as well as from faculty in their academic programs.[15] As instructional technologies are becoming more robust and the demand for academic preparation in youth development grows, more academic programs will undoubtedly turn to online learning opportunities to meet this demand.[16]

Field-based training

Increasing examples from the park and recreation field incorporate a blend of recreation and youth development competencies into regular staff trainings. For example, the Wheaton Park District in Illinois makes outcome-focused program development a team approach. Camp employees work together to develop program-specific goals and measurement tools to guide program-ming choices made throughout the summer. Staff goals may include providing parents with up-to-date information on daily activities, preparing methods to adapt activities to match the needs and abilities of all campers, or creating a fun environment where campers choose activities that match personal interests. Camper goals have included providing math improvement skills on a daily basis, improving each camper's ability to care for self and others, and developing campers' understanding and value of community service. Staff engage in these goal-setting sessions after having learned agency guidelines for planning and delivering recreation activities. Integrating youth development principles and practices into training helps the staff to be better prepared to provide youth-centered programs.

The Austin, Texas, Parks and Recreation Department uses certification programs and standards to balance worker competencies in both recreation and youth development. The department focuses on intentional programming with particular outcomes. Assistant director Kimberly McNeely sums up the organization's philosophy this way: "Whether we run basketball leagues, after-school or outdoor education programs, we must incorporate activities and methodologies that . . . intentionally . . . promote some youth development concept (self-esteem, future and mastery, cultural awareness, etc.)." Full-time employees plan and organize programs, while part-time staff are responsible for implementation and supervision. Realizing the benefits of a balanced approach to training, staff are exposed to recreation competencies, such as how to give directions, activity transition, and maintaining control of a group, along with dealing with behavioral issues. In addition, staff receive information on developmentally appropriate activities that can promote teamwork, leadership, and cooperation in support of outcome-focused programs.

Training park and recreation professionals on youth development principles is also happening on a higher, more collaborative level. In 2005, the Ohio Parks and Recreation Association presented the *Park and Recreation Program Leader Training Manual* to its constituent agencies contracted through a private company, Sports In Mind. The manual offers easy-to-follow directions for program supervisors to train frontline staff and volunteers. The immediate focus of the program is on the development of recreation programming competencies within agency employees. In addition, employees are instructed on how to have a positive effect on youth participants through communication, activity choice, and application of specific learning outcomes. By providing a comprehensive training guide, agencies can benefit from recognized standards and well-reviewed best practices.[17]

Conclusion

Recreation professionals have a long record of training staff through degree programs, accreditation, certification, and continuing education. However, much of that training is recreation specific and multigenerational in scope. Despite the fact that youth are often among the primary constituent groups for park and recreation agencies, youth development principles and practices are too often not considered in staff training and professional preparation for recreation workers. At the same time, youth development staff often use recreation activities as components of full-service youth development organizations, but they may lack information on basic recreation program design or activity leadership or may not have the expertise to choose and frame recreation activities in a developmentally appropriate way. We hope that bringing together the body of knowledge in both recreation and youth development can help to bridge these gaps.

Notes

1. Pittman, K., Irby, M., Tolman, J., Yohalem, N., & Ferber, T. (2003). *Preventing problems, promoting development, encouraging engagement: Competing priorities or inseparable goals?* Washington, DC: Forum for Youth Investment.

2. Witt, P. A., & Crompton, J. L. (2003). Positive youth development practices in recreation settings in the United States. *World Leisure Journal*, 45(2), 4–11; Schaumleffel, N. A., & Backlund, E. A. (2009). Program leaders'

intention to process recreation experiences to achieve targeted outcomes. *Managing Leisure, 14,* 141–160.

3. Astroth, K. A., Garza, P., & Taylor, B. (2004). Getting down to business: Defining competencies for entry-level youth workers. In P. Garza, L. Borden, & K. Astroth (Eds.). *Professional development for youth workers. New Directions for Youth Development, 104,* 25–37. San Francisco, CA: Jossey-Bass; Huebner, A., Walker, J., & MacFarland, M. (2003). Staff development for the youth development professional: A critical framework for understanding the work. *Youth and Society, 35*(2), 183–203.

4. Bocarro, J. N., & Barcelona, R. J. (2003). Come together: Unlocking the potential of collaboration between universities and park and recreation agencies. *Parks and Recreation, 38*(10), 50–55.

5. Astroth, Garza, & Taylor. (2004).

6. Sherman, C. P., Tran, C., & Alves, Y. (2010). Elementary school classroom teacher delivered physical education: Costs, benefits, and barriers. *Physical Educator, 67*(1), 2–17.

7. Eccles, J., & Gootman, J. A. (Eds.). (2002). *Community programs to promote youth development.* Washington, DC: National Academy Press.

8. Weiss, M. R., Bolter, N. D., Bhalla, J. A., & Price, M. S. (2007). Positive youth development through sport: Comparison of participants in The First Tee life skills programs with participants in other organized activities. *Journal of Sport and Exercise Psychology, 29*(Suppl.), S212; Debate, R. D., Gabriel, K. P., Zwald, M., Huberty, J., & Zhang, Y. (2009). Changes in psychosocial factors and physical activity frequency among third- to eighth-grade girls who participated in a developmentally focused youth sport program: A preliminary study. *Journal of School Health, 79*(10), 474–484.

9. Astroth et al. (2004). P. 27.

10. Quinn, J. (2004). Professional development in the youth development field: issues, trends, opportunities, and challenges. In P. Garza, L. Borden, & K. Astroth (Eds.), *Professional development for youth workers. New Directions for Youth Development, 104,* 13-24. San Francisco, CA: Jossey-Bass.

11. Astroth et al. (2004).

12. Hurd, A. (2005). Competency development for entry level public parks and recreation professionals. *Journal of Park and Recreation Administration, 23*(3), 45–62; Hurd, A. R., & Buschbom, T. (2010). Competency development for chief executive officers in YMCAs. *Managing Leisure, 15*(1), 96–110; Hammersley, C. H., & Tynon, J. F. (1998). Job competencies of entry level resort and commercial recreation professionals. *Journal of Applied Recreation Research, 23*(3), 225–241; Barcelona, B., & Ross, C. M. (2004). An analysis of the perceived competencies of recreational sports administrators. *Journal of Park and Recreation Administration, 22,* 25–42; Hurd, A. R., & McLean, D. D. (2004). An analysis of perceived competencies of CEOs in public parks and recreation agencies. *Managing Leisure, 9,* 96–110; Hurd, A. R. (2004). Competency development for board members in public park and recreation agencies. *Journal of Park and Recreation Administration, 22,* 43–61.

13. National Recreation and Park Association. (2004). Standards and evaluative criteria for baccalaureate programs in recreation, park resources, and

leisure services. Retrieved from http://nrpa.org/uploadedFiles/Learn_and_
Grow/Agency_Growth_Ops/COA_Standards%202004.pdf.

14. University of New Hampshire. (2008). *Adolescent and youth development
minor.* Retrieved from http://www.chhs.unh.edu/sites/chhs.unh.edu/files/
docs/fs/imf_Adolsecent_and_Youth_Development.pdf.

15. Barcelona, R. J. (2009). Pressing the online learning advantage: Commitment, content, and community. *Journal of Continuing Higher Education,*
57(3), 193–197.

16. Borden, L. M., Craig, D. L., & Villarruel, F. A. (2004). Professionaliz-
ing youth development: The role of higher education. In P. Garza, L. Borden,
& K. Astroth (Eds.), *Professional development for youth workers. New Directions
for Youth Development, 104,* 75–85.

17. Sports In Mind (2005). *Park and Recreation Program leader training manual.* Palm Harbor, FL: Author.

ROBERT J. BARCELONA *is an assistant professor in the College of Health,
Education, and Human Development at Clemson University.*

AMY R. HURD *is an associate professor in the School of Kinesiology and
Recreation at Illinois State University.*

JENNIFER A. BRUGGEMAN *is the cultural arts and teen supervisor for the
Wheaton (Illinois) Park District.*

Recreation has the potential to be an important public policy priority; however, it must be reframed to address critical policy priorities.

9

Reframing recreation as a public policy priority

Phillip Lovell

ISSUES PERTAINING TO children often struggle to become public policy priorities. A clear demonstration of this phenomenon is the degree to which children are supported in the federal budget in comparison to other priorities. Less than 10 percent of the federal budget is spent on children. In fact, the portion of federal spending focused on children has declined in the past five years from 8 percent in fiscal year (FY) 2006 to 7.79 percent in FY 2010.[1]

If issues pertaining to children struggle for the policy spotlight, subissues pertaining to them face an even greater challenge to be understood, valued, and ultimately prioritized by policymakers and addressed by public policy. Recreation undoubtedly falls under the latter category of subissues for several reasons. For the vast majority of policymakers, recreation is at best undefined, and its impact or goal is unclear. In short, from one perspective, recreation is a loosely defined means to an unclear end. In order for recreation to be included as an asset in public policy relating to children, it must be better understood as a healthy mix of positive opportunities that link to an array of positive outcomes for children, ranging from better health to success in education. This article describes the

NEW DIRECTIONS FOR YOUTH DEVELOPMENT, NO. 130, SUMMER 2011 © WILEY PERIODICALS, INC.
Published online in Wiley Online Library (wileyonlinelibrary.com) • DOI: 10.1002/yd.402

policy landscape into which recreation fits, suggests ways in which recreation can be reframed and recalibrated so that it can be positioned effectively as a policy priority, and suggests specific areas of public policy that practitioners and advocates can explore as avenues to expand the impact of positive recreational opportunities for children.

What is recreation?

The definitions of *recreation* are as diverse as the experiences children have while engaged in recreational activity. This is not helpful in the policy context, since it is difficult to incorporate an issue into policy if policymakers cannot clearly identify what is intended to be included in legislation, regulation, or other instruments of policy. For the purposes of this chapter, *recreation* is defined as a healthy mix of positive opportunities and experiences that link to an array of positive outcomes for children, ranging from better health to success in education. They are primarily selected by children and youth of their own accord, and they may be structured or unstructured. These opportunities may take place during school or nonschool hours, though they are more prevalent, and perhaps most important, during the approximately 40 percent of a young person's day spent outside of school.

Policy landscape

Of issues pertaining to children, two are most prevalent: children's health and education. Health reform legislation signed into law by President Barack Obama in 2010, the Patient Protection and Affordable Care Act (P.L. 111–148), contains several important provisions for children, including the extension of the Children's Health Insurance Program, funding for school-based health centers, and obesity prevention. The No Child Left Behind Act (P.L. 107–110) is the primary federal law governing education policy.

This legislation, the latest iteration of the Elementary and Secondary Education Act (ESEA), strives to strengthen public education by calling on states to set challenging academic standards for students and requiring students to be tested in mathematics and reading/language arts, in grades 3 to 8 and one time in high school. In FY 2010, federal spending in support of ESEA totaled nearly $25 billion.[2]

With the passage of the Patient Protection and Affordable Care Act, the primary opportunity for advancing recreation in federal policy lies in the area of education. At the time of this writing, the reauthorization (renewal and revision) of the ESEA is pending before Congress. Therefore, this article focuses on recreation as it pertains to education policy, with an emphasis on the reauthorization of ESEA.

Making recreation relevant to federal policy

Those in the field of recreation may maintain that quality recreational opportunities for young people, and the assets they contribute toward positive youth development, are of intrinsic value. Viewing recreation as a vehicle for positive youth development, one may associate recreation with assets developed in such categories as physical health, cognitive development, psychological and emotional development, and social development.[3] Seeing these assets as beneficial, if not necessary, for children to become successful adults, it would logically follow that policymakers should value recreation and embed it in federal policy relating to children.

Positive youth development, however, has yet to emerge as a concept that federal policymakers value. This is evident in the nation's lack of an overarching youth policy, the bifurcation of federal programs across myriad federal departments and agencies,[4] and the relatively few references to "positive youth development" within federal laws and regulations relating to children and youth.

Therefore, relating recreation to the field of positive youth development in the effort to position recreation as a policy priority

NEW DIRECTIONS FOR YOUTH DEVELOPMENT • DOI: 10.1002/yd

is unlikely to create a convincing argument to policymakers. Policymakers must understand that recreation is directly relevant to outcomes and priorities that are of value to them. One such policy priority is education.

Connecting recreation to federal education policy

Directly connecting recreation to education policy may be uncomfortable to recreation proponents associated with the perspective that the assets directly developed through positive recreational experiences are of intrinsic value and need not be tied to the field of education or any other area in order to demonstrate its value. With regard to the recreation-education connection specifically, hesitation may rise because of the perception that education policy is overly focused on test-based accountability. Recreation practitioners are unlikely to want to engage young people in activities that are expected to produce increases in standardized test scores. A counterargument to this concern is threefold.

First, since positive recreational experiences develop myriad strengths in young people, associating recreation with academic impacts is one way practitioners can be intentional about recognizing, and communicating, the broad range of outcomes that can directly and indirectly result from quality recreation.

Second, intentionally connecting recreational experiences to academic experiences and outcomes could greatly expand the opportunity for young people to participate in recreation. For example, the number of schools identified for improvement under the No Child Left Behind (NCLB) Act is growing and will continue to grow. Eighteen million students attend schools in school districts that are failing according to NCLB, and the number of districts required to undergo corrective action, one of the most rigorous categories of NCLB's accountability system, increased fivefold in the most recent two years for which data are available (from 2005–2006 to 2006–2007).[5] By using recreational opportunities as a way to help increase student achievement, many students, including large numbers of students from traditionally underserved communities, may be able to benefit from experiences that heretofore have largely been the purview of more affluent segments of the student population.

Third, the academic performance of American students is dangerously low. Roughly one-quarter of students fail to graduate on time, and for students of color, on-time graduation is nearly a fifty-fifty proposition.[6] This will have a detrimental impact on the nation and its economy. By 2018, two-thirds of jobs will require some postsecondary education, and there is a projected shortfall of 3 million workers with the necessary education to fill these positions.[7] If connecting students, particularly low-performing students, with positive recreational experiences can help to increase their academic performance, there is a moral and economic imperative to do so.

Opportunities for expanding recreational opportunities within federal policy

The current fiscal and political climates do not necessarily lend themselves to new ideas and approaches for serving children and youth. New federal resources are likely to be limited in the short term, forcing recreation practitioners and advocates to be proactive and creative regarding identifying potential options for expanding recreation through federal policy. This notwithstanding, there are several opportunities for doing so.

Common Core State Standards Initiative. States have worked together to develop a set of common academic standards that will prepare students for college and careers. The Common Core State Standards Initiative, coordinated by the Council of Chief State School Officers and the National Governors Association Center for Best Practices, has produced standards that "define the knowledge and skills students should have within their K-12 education careers so that they will graduate high school able to succeed in entry-level, credit-bearing academic college courses and in workforce training programs."[8] This endeavor will help to address one of the most significant and unintentional repercussions of NCLB: the lowering of state standards in order to increase the number of students achieving at proficient levels as required under the law.

Federal education policy encouraged the adoption of the common core by providing points in the Department of Education's Race to the Top competition to states adopting the common core. By December 2010, more than forty states and the District of Columbia had adopted the common core standards in English language arts and mathematics.

The widespread adoption of the common core standards provides an important opportunity for recreation practitioners. Specifically, states, school districts, and schools will be implementing these standards over the next several years. As recreation programs and strategies are developed and revised, they can be designed to support students in achieving the common core. Doing so would simultaneously help students while making recreation opportunities directly relevant to the education community.

21st Century Community Learning Centers. Among current federal funding opportunities, the 21st Century Community Learning Centers (21st CCLC) program is likely to be the most significant source supporting recreational activities: it provides federal funding for programming during out-of-school time to low-performing students in low-performing schools. Funding for this program increased from $981 million in 2006 to $1.17 billion in 2010.

The Obama administration proposed expanding the use of 21st CCLC funds for extended learning time in its budget proposal for FY 2011 and FY 2012.[9] The proposed 2011 omnibus appropriations bill included an increase for this program of $135 million and would expand the availability of funding to extended learning programs that include school-community partnerships and provide enrichment opportunities. The final "continuing resolution" funding the government for FY 2011 included neither the proposed funding increase nor these proposed policy changes. Still, the proposed increase in funding, combined with the requirement that extended learning opportunities be implemented through partnerships between school districts and community based organizations, demonstrates that 21st CCLC is likely to continue to be a potential funding source for quality recreation opportunities.

Promoting SUCCESS Act (Promoting Students Using the Camp Community for Enrichment, Strength, and Success). The Promoting SUCCESS Act is proposed to be included in the reauthorization of ESEA. It would provide grants from the Department of Education to for-profit organizations, nonprofit organizations, and school districts in order to reduce childhood obesity and strengthen graduation rates by reducing summer learning loss. This would be achieved through a balanced array of activities offered during the summer, beginning with the summer after grade 5 through the summer before grade 10. Activities would be provided in the areas of academic support, health and wellness, independent living, environmental stewardship, and leadership development. Measures of success would include increases in the number of students performing at the proficient level in core academic subjects, developmental outcomes ranging from leadership and civic engagement to responsibility and independence, and the participation of students in moderate to vigorous physical activity.

The Promoting SUCCESS Act fills a significant gap in federal policy regarding summer learning loss. Research demonstrates that summer learning loss accumulates as students matriculate from grade to grade, so much so that by the time students enter the ninth grade, many are so far off-track that on-time graduation from high school becomes a near impossibility.[10] If enacted and funded, the Promoting SUCCESS Act provides an opportunity to specifically support quality recreational experiences for children and measure the impact of such experiences.

School Improvement Grants. School Improvement Grants (SIG), authorized under the No Child Left Behind Act, received a significant infusion of funding through the American Recovery and Reinvestment Act (ARRA), commonly referred to as the economic stimulus package. The purpose of the program is to turn around the nation's lowest-performing schools. Between 2007 and 2010, funding for this program rose from $125 million to $546 million. As part of ARRA, an additional $3 billion was provided to this program.

The Department of Education issued regulations guiding the implementation of SIG in 2010. Schools receiving SIG funds are required to implement one of four reform models: turnaround, transformation, restart, or closure. Public attention has focused on the elements of these reform models requiring teacher and principal replacement, the closure of low-performing schools, and the conversion of low-performing schools to charter schools. Much less attention has been paid to provisions of the regulations beyond these controversial elements, including provisions that may provide opportunities for recreation.

For example, under the turnaround model, the Department of Education requires school districts to provide "appropriate social-emotional and community-oriented services and supports for students." Under the transformation model, school districts are required to provide "ongoing mechanisms for family and community engagement" and may partner with organizations "to create safe school environments that meet students' social, emotional, and health needs."[11]

While recreation is not specifically included in the regulations, the repeated references to social and emotional services and needs, as well as references to partnerships, open the door to innovative recreation practitioners to develop or strengthen relationships with school districts to provide students with a well-rounded educational and developmental experience.

No child left inside. Similar to the Promoting SUCCESS Act, the No Child Left Inside Act is proposed to be included in the ESEA reauthorization. Under the legislation, states would develop environmental literacy plans, professional development would be provided toward the development and implementation of environmental education curricula, and national grants would be provided to strengthen the capacity of practitioners to implement environmental education. At the close of the 111th session of Congress in 2010, the No Child Left Inside Act had the support of 124 members of the House of Representatives and 20 senators.

This proposal would integrate environmental education into the public education system. For example, states would have to develop content standards on environmental education and describe how the state's plan connects to high school graduation requirements. In addition, funding would be available for evaluating the impact of environmental education on academic achievement and graduation rates. If included in the ESEA, the No Child Left Inside Act could open an array of opportunities for recreational activities that focus on environmental stewardship.

Conclusion

Reframing recreation as a public policy priority is critical for the field, yet not without its challenges. Because few policymakers understand the value and benefits of recreation, practitioners and advocates must closely connect recreation to issues that are of concern to policymakers. A significant policy opportunity to expand recreational opportunities for children and youth lies in the area of education, including ESEA reauthorization. By educating policymakers on the myriad outcomes that can result from quality recreational experiences and by developing and implementing such proposals as those described in this article, solid, incremental progress can be made in positioning recreation as a public policy priority.

Notes

1. These figures do not include spending from the American Recovery and Reinvestment Act (ARRA). If spending from ARRA is included, the portion of the fiscal year 2010 budget dedicated to children is 8.7 percent, still less than 10 percent of the federal budget. First Focus. (2010). *Children's budget 2010.* Washington, DC: Author.

2. U.S. Department of Education. (2010). *Fiscal year 2011 education budget summary and background information.* Washington, DC: Author.

3. These are the categories of assets outlined by the National Research Council's Board on Children, Youth, and Families in its seminal publication: *Community programs to promote youth development.* National Research Council and Institute of Medicine. (2002). *Community programs to promote youth development.* Washington, DC: National Academy Press.

4. For more on the notion of a comprehensive approach to federal youth policy, see White House Task Force for Disadvantaged Youth. (2003).

White House Task Force for Disadvantaged Youth final report. Washington, DC: Author.

5. U.S. Department of Education, Office of Planning, Evaluation and Policy Development, Policy and Program Studies Service. (2010, August). *State and local implementation of the No Child Left Behind Act: Volume IX. Accountability under* NCLB: *Final report.* Washington, DC: Author.

6. The national graduation rate is 74 percent. Eighty percent of white students graduate on time, whereas 60 percent of black students and 62 percent of Hispanic students graduate on time. Aud, S., Fox, M., & Kewal Ramani, A. (2010). *Status and trends in the education of racial and ethnic groups.* Washington, DC: U.S. Government Printing Office.

7. Carnevale, A. P., Smith, N., & Strohl, J. (2010). *Help wanted: Projections of jobs and education requirements through 2018.* Washington, DC: Georgetown University Center on Education and the Workforce.

8. Common Core State Standards Initiative. *About the standards.* January, 2011. Retrieved from http://www.corestandards.org/about-the-standards.

9. U.S. Department of Education. (2010); and U.S. Department of Education. (2011). *Fiscal year 2012 education budget summary and background information.* Washington, DC: Author.

10. Alexander, K. L., Entwisle, D. R., & Steffel Olson, L. (2007). Lasting consequences of the summer learning gap. *American Sociological Review, 72,* 167–180.

11. School Improvement Grants; American Recovery and Reinvestment Act of 2009 (ARRA); Title I of the Elementary and Secondary Education Act of 1965, as Amended (ESEA). 75 Fed. Reg. 66367–66371, October, 28, 2010.

PHILLIP LOVELL *is a member of the Public Policy Committee of the American Camp Association board of directors.*

Index